Changing Lives:
women, inclusion and the PhD

Changing Lives:
women, inclusion and the PhD

*Edited by Barbara Ann Cole
and Helen M Gunter*

Trentham Books
Stoke on Trent, UK and Sterling, USA

Trentham Books Limited
Westview House   22883 Quicksilver Drive
734 London Road   Sterling
Oakhill   VA 20166-2012
Stoke on Trent   USA
Staffordshire
England ST4 5NP

First published 2010

British Library Cataloguing-in-Publication Data
A catalogue record for this book is available from the British Library

ISBN 978 1 85856 461 6

Thanks to Taylor & Francis for permission for extract from 'Students as Stakeholders' by Karin Oelermans in *Journal of Educational Administration and History* vol 39 no1.

Designed and typeset by Trentham Books Ltd and printed in Great Britain by Cpod Ltd, Trowbridge.

Contents

The Contributors

Penny Jane Burke is Professor of Education at Roehampton University. Her contribution to widening participation is reflected in the range of her work. Dedicated to creating spaces for dialogue across theory and practice, she designed the innovative course 'Widening Participation: Policy and Practice'. Her sole-authored book, *Accessing Education: effectively widening participation* (2002), draws on her ethnographic study of mature students' experiences of accessing lifelong learning opportunities. Her co-authored book *Reconceptualising Lifelong Learning: Feminist Interventions* (Burke and Jackson, 2007) was nominated for the 2008 Cyril O. Houle World Award for Outstanding Literature in Adult Education. Penny received the Higher Education Academy's prestigious National Teaching Fellowship award in 2008 and is the Access and Widening Participation Network Leader for the Society for Research in Higher Education (SRHE).

Barbara Cole is currently Faculty Director of Post Graduate Research and senior lecturer in Inclusive Education at the Institute of Education, University of London. She is a member of the editorial board of the *International Journal of Inclusive Education*. Barbara has worked in both mainstream secondary schools and FE, before moving into HE, and has worked in a number of different locations including the Caribbean and Singapore. Her research interests include inclusion and exclusion in educational contexts; the relationships between parents and professionals; and the use of narrative to explore intersections of gender and disability and experiences of inclusion and exclusion. She won the TES/NASEN award for best academic book 2005 with *Mother-Teachers: Insights into Inclusion* (2004).

Gloria Gordon, a 2002 National Teaching Fellow, is senior lecturer in the Department of Management, Faculty of Business at London South Bank University. She is also Research Director for the Centre for British African Caribbean Studies (CBACS), founded in 2007 with the purpose of applying knowledge to the life experience of descendants of enslaved Africans. Author of *Towards Bicultural Competence: Beyond Black and White* (2007), Gloria has recently added the Formative Learning Centre (FLC) to CBACS' portfolio, making a significant contribution to not only ending the problems of black Caribbean educational underachievement in Britain but also enhancing the overall learning experience of students more generally.

Helen Gunter is Professor of Educational Policy, Leadership and Management in the School of Education, University of Manchester. She has produced over seventy publications including books and papers on leadership theory and practice, and she co-edits the *Journal of Educational Administration and History.* Her work has focused education policy and the growth of school leadership, where she has used Bourdieu's thinking tools to explain the configuration and development of the field. She is particularly interested in its history, particularly developments in knowledge production. Recently she completed the Knowledge Production in Educational Leadership Project funded by the ESRC, where she studied the relationship between the state, public policy and knowledge, and she is about to begin a project on Distributed Leadership funded by the ESRC with her colleagues Dave Hall and Joanna Bragg.

Kate Hoskins is currently lecturer on the MSc Youth Participation at Birkbeck College, University of London. She also lectures and supervises students on the MA in Education Studies at London Metropolitan University. Kate completed a Master's degree in Education and Social Policy at King's College London and is now undertaking a PhD there, entitled 'Senior female academics in the English Academy: A classed and gendered exploration of success' in the Policy Studies Centre. Kate's current research interests include understanding how senior female academics experience their objective career success. Forthcoming publications include, 'The Price of Success? The experiences of four Senior Working Class Female Academics in the UK' (*Women's Studies International Forum*).

Jennifer Lavia is a lecturer and director of Caribbean Programmes at the University of Sheffield, School of Education. Her current research interests include perspectives of the colonised, transnational identities and transformative educational practice. She also studies Caribbean education systems. Her forthcoming publication (2010), edited with Michelle Moore is *Cross-Cultural Perspectives on Policy and Practice: Decolonizing community contexts.*

Heidi Safia Mirza is Professor of Equalities Studies in Education and Director of the Centre for Equalities, Rights and Social Justice (CRESJ) at the Institute of Education, University of London. She attended Goldsmith's College, University of London where she completed her PhD in 1988, entitled, 'The Career Aspirations and Expectations of Young Black Women: The Maintenance of Inequality'. She is known internationally for her work on ethnicity, gender and identity in education and established the Runnymede Collection, an archive documenting the history of the civil rights struggle for a multicultural Britain. She is author of several books including *Young Female and Black*, and *Race Gender and Educational Desire*, and the seminal collections *Black British Feminism and Black and Postcolonial Feminisms in New Times.*

Acknowledgements

This book has its origins in the lives, studies and achievements of the people directly involved, and those who have helped and hindered. As editors we would like to thank Jennifer, Gloria, Penny, Heidi and Kate for their involvement in the project and for sharing such a large part of their experiences. We have been enriched by knowing and working with them, and we hope to keep the dialogue going as we move off into the next phase of our work and lives. We would also like to thank Trentham Books, especially Gillian Klein for her support and encouragement particularly in the early stages of the project. We would also like to acknowledge the very important initial conversation we shared with Professor Richard Bates which greatly stimulated our thinking and helped to develop our ideas. Of course we take full responsibility for the book and any weaknesses are entirely ours. Last but not least we would like to thank Mike and Barry for their everlasting patience, for listening, and for being themselves.

1

New Beginnings – Ongoing Lives

Barbara Ann Cole and Helen M Gunter

Introduction: the aims of the book

> You must learn to use your life experiences in your intellectual work: continually to examine it and interpret it. In this sense craftsmanship is the centre of yourself and you are personally involved in every intellectual product upon which you work. (Mills, 1970:216)

When these words of Mills were published in the *Sociological Imagination*, Barbara was a second year history undergraduate and Helen was a young schoolgirl. Neither of us had any knowledge or understanding of how these words would come to life for us or for the other contributors to this book. Yet as the autobiographical narratives in this book illustrate, we have all, in different ways and for different reasons, developed our professional academic lives from and through our own personal histories and experiences and continue to strive to do so.

Why and how we became academics was not necessarily something we initially sought, but was rather a result of diverse and sometimes colliding circumstances, events and histories. As is evidenced in the chapters to follow, this was sometimes an uncomfortable and challenging experience. Yet this book is not about the phoenix emerging from the ashes. The stories told here are not tales of woe or hardship. Nor are they intended as heroic examples of good prevailing over adversity. The book is not an attempt to suggest that embarking on doctoral study is a

1

panacea for all ills. On the contrary it tells the journeys of six women who have drawn on their own lived experiences to complete doctoral studies and gone on to develop careers in which they continue to build on their beliefs in educational and social inclusion in related but different fields of sociological study.

While there has been little written to date about the experiences of women in higher education, the field can be said to date back to 1866, when Emily Davis, founder of Girton College, Cambridge, wrote about the *Higher Education of Women*. The last thirty years have seen a small but growing literature around experiences of higher education but, according to Leonard (2001:2), little work has been done on the gender differences or experiences between men and women regarding research degrees, despite the developing literature around gender and the labour market, and the differences in achievement between girls and boys in schools. Leonard goes on to state:

> even less attention has been given to differences among women and men postgraduate students: between those who study full-time and those who study part-time, between those in different disciplines, between those who do their doctorates immediately after their first degree and 'mature' women returners', between those who have lived all their lives in Britain and those whose 'domicile' is abroad or whose first language is not English, between lesbians and heterosexuals, who are single or in couples, with and without children, with and without disabilities, and so on. (Leonard, 2001:2)

While this book does not claim to consider all these issues it does seek to examine one particular group of mature women returners from a diversity of backgrounds and experiences. It offers the narratives of six women who have undertaken doctoral studies at different stages of their personal and professional lives. It is not a 'how to do' doctoral research book, but we hope it will have a place in the reading of prospective, current and past students; for the women, and men, who are thinking of embarking on a higher degree or who have already begun doctoral study, and that it will resonate with those who have completed their studies. We hope it will make connections with those who teach and work with doctoral students and offer further insights into their work and relationships with the men and women who bring diverse and complex experiences and emotions to their academic study.

In this time of potential economic hardship for many and of policy debates about funding and higher education, we hope it will also be read by those who formulate policy at government level. The personal and professional struggles and difficulties encountered by many doctoral students are completely missing from the official statistics and accounts. Although completion rates are published and regarded as relevant to the success or otherwise of HE institutions, the personal and gendered stories behind them are rarely told or even acknowledged, and their importance remains largely unrecognised. Leonard argues that what is written about women and higher education is done from the perspectives of faculty and policy makers rather than of students, 'full of references in a typically academic way, to convince people about the importance of gender' and are not, therefore, 'particularly easy reading' (Leonard, 2001:2). In her book, Leonard aims to 'speak directly to any woman who is going to undertake a doctorate' and gives research-based information on how women are positioned inequitably within the supposedly liberal, cerebral world of postgraduate studies. She suggests that women are not only less likely to be invited to do a research degree but may even 'brush off the recognition' (2001:4). Women need to know about what Leonard refers to as 'the informal rules' and 'informal structures' and be able to recognise what 'counts' in academic life. Arguably, such knowledge can emerge from personal experiential accounts.

So we hope the book will also be of interest to social scientists who want to engage with narrative and the story genre and the use of conceptual tools regarding explanations of practice and change. The stories will be a resource for supporting doctoral research in particular and research activity generally, and will enable active researchers as well as professionals on a range of professional development and Masters courses to consider how to locate the self productively within projects.

Context, complexity and contradiction are central issues in the book. In her chapter, Barbara examines her own and her son's experiences amidst policies of educational inclusion and those promoting a quasi-market and standards agenda in education. It has been argued that this has resulted in contradictions and tensions for many children and their families as well as for teachers and schools (Barton, 1998; Gillborn and Youdell, 2000; Cole, 2004). Such contradiction appears to abound in current education policy thinking and appears increasingly to be a part of higher education. While the main focus of the standards agenda has so far been schools, government policy regarding standards now seems to be shifting to HE institutions, with calls for a range of measures to evaluate quality in universities and for the development of national standards, inspection and regulation.

At the same time, amidst rising unemployment, particularly among the young, the government has set out targets for up to fifty percent of young people to attend university, despite the threat of raising tuition fees for students and poorer prospects of employment on completion. Despite such policy tensions, it remains evident that the number of mature students in HE is increasing, as is the number of women completing doctoral study. Also evident from the literature is the significant increase in the number of women in higher education (Leonard, 2001) and this is not restricted to the UK. For the 7430 women and 5710 men who completed part time and full time doctoral studies in 2007/8 (HESA, 2007-8), there will be many complex individual and collective stories to tell against a background of changing education policy background. Such experiences might reveal the kinds of knowledge Leonard writes about.

This book seeks to offer broader insights than Leonard suggests. While we cannot claim to have shared all the experiences of our students, we have all completed doctoral research. We are all female academics within UK higher education institutions. We are all doctoral supervisors ourselves, who know the emotional, financial, professional and personal difficulties which can impact on a student and change their priorities. At the same time we have all attended degree award ceremonies and shared with the families and friends the joy as students receive their degrees, recognising the individual and joint endeavours and sacrifices of students and their families along the journey. The narratives told in this book are all very different yet they all reflect the ebb and flow of life and the changing policy, sociological contexts and the importance of both continuities and change. In this opening chapter we want to explore some of the themes and issues which both underpin and emerge from our narratives.

Themes which emerged in the book

Embarking on doctoral research can be one way of creating new and different roles and constructions of self, as the narratives here suggest. Beginning such a journey can reflect the challenges and changes going on in other areas of life and it may be affected by them. In and of itself it can also bring about changes in the lives of students and their families, introducing new complexities, new ways of thinking and of perceiving the world which can be challenging for all concerned. In this sense, change is a major theme and the book offers an opportunity to examine what it means to experience such life changes in ways that speak to a range of people at different stages in their lives, careers and studies.

Diversity is another important underlying theme for while, the six authors are all female and are now academics in UK higher education institutions, their origins, family histories, routes to and through academia have many differences as well as commonalities. None of them followed a so-called traditional route through from undergraduate study, to higher degree to a professional life in academia, without struggle, challenge and change along the way. Often this emanated from or resulted in huge personal or professional challenges. For all of us there have been elements of serendipity in this development: of being in a particular place at a particular moment in time; of our own histories emerging from those of our mothers, grandmothers and forbears, but at the same time of being located in a different time and space.

The importance of context is another essential element. All the authors grew up in societies and communities responding to the challenges of the last fifty or so years, including the 'sexual revolution' of the 1960s, feminism, postmodernism and post-structuralism, post-colonialism, globalisation, multiculturalism, changing constructions of the family and the gender roles within them, including changing perceptions of women in the workplace, widening participation, and educational and social inclusion. Political, social and economic changes have all affected the lives re-presented here and have informed the context of our individual and collective personal and professional experiences. Through our accounts we have attempted to reflect the significance of context and the political, historical and sociological changes taking place over the last fifty years.

In her book, Marianne Gullestad (1996) writes:

> I hope to show that 'ordinary people' relate in creative and complex ways to structural conditions and to social categories, labels, and concepts associated with such conditions. There is a dynamic relationship between hegemonic values – transmitted through institutions such as schools, churches, and mass media – and individual efforts at making sense of what goes on around them ... The overall problem of this book can be put as a question of what human beings receive from other people, and how they creatively refashion and adapt knowledges, values, and ideas, they receive ... Traditions are not just inherited; individuals choose among elements and make them theirs in processes of active construction and reconstruction. People live out their lives and tell their stories within socially structured conditions, but their actions and stories also have a potentially transforming impact on 'society'. (1996:31-32)

Gullestad maintains that when 'grand' narratives lose their power, smaller narratives gain credence, for example autobiography. We have to live with tensions and contradictions, ambiguities, paradoxes and dilemmas and to seek our answers not in binaries but in integration and inclusion. Gullestad highlights the importance of creating different combinations of identities and roles through more pluralistic constructions of self.

The tensions and complexities noted by Gullestad are certainly recognised in much feminist research. Indeed, many feminists maintain that it is not gender alone which marginalises women but the complexities and multiple interactions between gender and other categories such as race, disability, class, religion, faith, poverty, age and so on (Sheldon, 2004; Collins, 2000; hooks, 2000; Thomas, 1999). Increasingly, this interaction is referred to as 'intersectionality', a term originally used by Kimberlé Crenshaw (1989) to acknowledge how the experiences of Black women fell between the separate discourses of gender and race. More recently intersectionality has been described as:

> the interaction between gender, race and other categories of difference in individual lives, social practices, institutional arrangements, and cultural ideologies and the outcomes of these interactions in terms of power. (Davis, 2008:68)

Intersectionality is now acknowledged as one of the most important feminist contributions to understanding the different experiences of women (McCall, 2005; Davis, 2008).

According to Davis, intersectionality, as a 'good feminist theory' alerts us to the idea that the

> ... world around us is always more complicated and contradictory than we ever could have anticipated. ... It encourages each feminist scholar to engage critically with her own assumptions in the interests of reflexive, critical, and accountable feminist inquiry. (Davis, 2008:79)

Intersectionality brings together two significant aspects of feminist thinking; firstly, the impact of race, class and gender (amongst others) on women's lives, and how relations of power are produced and transformed through this interaction within women's lives and experiences. Secondly, it offers support for the deconstruction of binaries, normalisation theories and homogenising categories while simultaneously offering a platform which can address the concerns of all women (Davis, 2008:71-72). Davis writes:

> It promises an almost universal applicability, useful for understanding and analysing any social practice, any individual or group experience, any structural arrangement, and any cultural configuration. Moreover, it can – by definition – be employed by any (feminist) scholar willing to use her own social location, whatever it may be, as an analytic resource rather than just an identity marker. (Davis, 2008:71-72)

It is probable that intersectionality will provide a continuing source of discussion for the future amongst feminists for, uniquely, it brings critical feminist theory about the impact of race, class and sexism on gender together with post structural feminist critical methodology seeking to deconstruct categories. It provides a collaborative platform for different feminist researchers and theorists (Davis, 2008). While there may still be some discussion around what intersectionality is (theory, heuristic device or reading strategy); how it should be conceptualised (as 'axes of difference' or 'dynamic process'); whether it concerns individual experience, theorising or identity; or is a 'property of social structures and cultural discourses' (Davis, 2008:68), it is the ambiguity of intersectionality which is its strength, for 'with each new intersection, new connections emerge and previously hidden exclusions come to light' (Davis, 2008:77).

We hope the chapters in this book offer the reader opportunities to explore different intersections. Heidi Mirza, Jennifer Lavia and Gloria

Gordon reflect on their own racialised and gendered experiences in a slowly changing post-colonial world. Helen Gunter tells of the educational opportunities almost denied to her as a working class northern girl but ultimately offered by the introduction of comprehensive education. Penny Jane Burke examines her personal experiences of exclusion and then inclusion through gender studies. She describes her determination as a young mother in a foreign country to access higher education and the opportunities this offered, which emerged through a widening participation agenda. Barbara Ann Cole reflects on the impact of social pressures to conform to classed and gendered norms amidst the sexual revolution of the 1960s; the expectations to achieve at school and in higher education but not to do too well; to be good but not too good to ultimately marry and have a family, and most definitely in that order. Such things were the givens of middle class family life, the so-called 'unchallenged' which, according to Foucault, should be challenged:

> It is a matter of pointing out on what kinds of assumptions, what kinds of familiar, unchallenged modes of thought the practices we accept rest ... flushing out that thought and trying to change it: to show that things are not as self-evident as one believed, to see that what is accepted as self-evident will no longer be accepted as such ... In these circumstances, criticism (and radical criticism) is absolutely indispensable for any transformation ... As soon as one can no longer think things as one formerly thought them, transformation becomes both very urgent, very difficult and quite possible. (Foucault in Kritzman, 1988:154)

Sawicki suggests that perhaps the 'least dangerous way to discover whether and how specific practices are enslaving or liberating us is not to silence and exclude differences, but rather to use them to diversify and renegotiate the arena of radical political struggle' (Sawicki, 1991: 48). Yet until the last decades of the 20th century stories such as the ones in this book were not heard and women's voices generally were missing from the public forum and consequently from history. Dorothy Smith claims that women have been 'living in an intellectual, cultural and political world from whose making we have been almost entirely excluded and in which we had been recognised as no more than marginal voices' (Smith, 1987:1). Since the 1960s and 1970s there has been a great deal of feminist research which has considered the changing role of women as mothers, workers and professionals within the 'massive social transformations in family life, through economic and social changes on an increasingly global scale over the last fifty years' (David, 2000:11). But she argues that while education has changed women's lives, the changes have not been reflected in public policies or employment (David, 2000).

In our attempt to counter the marginalisation referred to by Smith (1987), we have chosen to draw on what are sometimes referred to as personal experience approaches, involving what Ellis and Bochner (2000) call 'evocative narratives' (p744).

Personal experience approaches or 'evocative narratives'

Reflective narrative research characterises the concept of this book. It relates not only to the means by which the stories have been gathered and presented, but also to the substantive issues considered. Within the social sciences, the PhD process is very reflective. If you are considering embarking on doctoral studies, or have already done so, you will no doubt at some time have asked yourself why! Why have you taken on this project at this time in your life? What are the costs, not just in terms of time and money, but in relation to you, your family, friends, your professional life and other commitments? Relating back to the opening words of Mills, how are your 'life experiences' involved in your intellectual work and how will the craftsmanship you bring reflect them?

New researchers often believe that quantitative, positivist research is what they should be doing because the relative methodological safety of terms such as reliability, objectivity and validity can be found in such research. This is not the place to discuss the different merits of quantitative or qualitative research: such a discussion can be found in most texts about research methods. Suffice to say that in this book the contributors have deliberately chosen to take a qualitative, feminist, narrative research approach, in which positionality, voice, lived experiences, values and beliefs are all integral.

Perhaps our choice of methodology is best explained by Art Bochner. He argues for a more personal and interactive relationship between researchers, subjects, authors and reader focuses on personal experience, which is

... endowed with meaning and on the moral and ethical choices we face as human beings who live in an uncertain and changing world. I also wanted to understand the conventions that constrain which stories we can tell and how we can tell them, and to show how people can and do resist the forms of social control that marginalise or silence counter narratives, ... stories that create the effect of reality, showing characters embedded in the complexities of lived moments of struggle, resisting the intrusions of chaos, disconnection, fragmentation, marginalisation, and incoherence, trying to preserve or restore the continuity and coherence of life's unity in the face of unexpected blows of fate that call one's meanings and values into question. I refer to these personal stories as evocative narratives. ...Usually the author of an evocative narrative writes in the first person, making herself the object of the research and thus breaching the conventional, separation of researcher and subjects (Jackson, 1989); the story often focuses on a single case and thus breaches the traditional concerns of research from generalisation across cases to generalisation within a case (Geertz, 1973); ... the disclosure of hidden details of private life challenges the rational actor model of social performance; the narrative text refuses the impulse to abstract and explain, stressing the journey over the destination, and thus eclipses the scientific illusion of control and mastery; and the episodic portrayal of the ebb and flow of relationship experience dramatises the motion of connected lives across the curve of time... (Ellis and Bochner, 2000:744)

Personal experience methods are not new (see Hatch and Wisniewski, 1995). They are increasingly being seen as an important method of analysis in the social sciences (Clandinin, 2007; Josselson and Lieblich, 1999; Polkinghorne, 1995; Plummer, 1993; Denzin, 1989). Clandinin and Connelly (1994:425) use the term 'personal experience methods' to emphasise the personal nature of narrative research and the 'fundamental human connection among us'. Through such narratives we organise our experiences into 'temporarily meaningful episodes' (Robertson, 1999:69), and try to make our lives more coherent and understandable (Richardson, 1990:10; see also Gorelick, 1991; Sparkes, 1994). Emihovich (1995) argues that storying the data enables it to link emotion and reason and to survive the moment in which it is told.

Yet narrative is not without its critics and important issues are being debated. There are concerns around terminology and definitions: are these stories, life stories, life histories, narratives, accounts or other? (see Goodson and Sikes, 2001). Can others 'give voice' and can doing so confine the teller within their own perceptions, offering them nothing they don't already know? Can such narratives initiate change? How are such stories to be analysed, evaluated – or should they 'speak for themselves' (Van Maanen, 1988:19)? There is also a danger of fixing the story in time and place while time moves on. However, one of the seeming strengths of narrative is that it can speak beyond its own time, retaining its complexity (Polkinghorne, 1995:11). Another claim for narrative is that such approaches are recognised as being characterised by deep respect for the perceptions of the participants and understandings and meaning-making of lived experience (Van Manen, 1990).

The narrators in this collection have all struggled to tell just one story for, as Polkinghorne reminds us, we are 'in middle of our stories and cannot be sure how they will end; we are constantly having to revise the plot as new events are added to our lives' (Polkinghorne, 1988:150). While they may be 'subject to incompleteness, personal bias and selective recall' (Butt *et al*, 1992:91), the stories told here are the ones we choose to tell here and now. We share with Art Bochner the view that the telling of such narratives is important. The alternative might be *enforced* silence.

Reflecting back to the opening words of Mills again, Liz Stanley (1993) also reminds us of the importance of the auto/biography of the researcher in carrying out and interpreting fieldwork and data indeed in the whole conceptualisation of the research project. And Coffey argues that as researchers we need to understand and acknowledge 'how the self gets written into accounts of fieldwork' (Coffey, 1999:115).

These stories are not presented as examples of the 'naïve incompetent overcoming adversity and difficulty, in the quest for data' (Coffey, 1999: 125), but rather the writing establishes what Coffey refers to as the 'interconnectedness' between the field and the self; the process of writing thereby adds 'critical reflection to our ongoing task of making sense out of who we are and what it is that we do' (Agar, 1986:xi quoted in Coffey, 1999). Coffey argues that:

> The positionality of the self is the starting point for such accounts. The narratives of the self parallel, and to some extent consume, the narratives of the field. The selves that are constructed and written are complex and relational. They are not research instruments, or props. Rather they are gendered,

racialised, sexualised, embodied and emotional. In contrast to fieldnotes (which are often private) and the partial autobiographical accounts (which are usually orientated to the research process), ethnographic writing which locates the self as central, gives analytic purchase to the autobiographical. (Coffey, 1999:126)

The six stories

The book presents six stories and locates them in the context in which the study has been undertaken. This means that not only the person is under scrutiny in relation to the reasons to embark on study but also the historical setting in which the structures operate to shape decisions. This reveals issues about social movements, not least post-colonial thinking combined with gender identity in a changing world; personal and professional vulnerabilities and communities. The interplay between lives as lived with the living life of entering academia is a key feature of the stories, making the book essential reading for all those who are about to embark on academic study as well as those who have completed it. Study does not always come out of smooth linear lives and all readers will be able to relate to these stories. This will enable researchers to think about and engage with the authoring of their identities. The book not only presents the stories but also troubles them through the use of conceptual tools regarding the self, others and the narration of stories.

We are certainly not arguing that women should get a Doctorate in order to change themselves or change others in what Leonard refers to as in the 'woman's magazine' mould (2001:6). Rather, the narratives reflect the very personal accounts, experiences and struggles of individual women. They are contextualised within current relevant policies and within the historical and sociological contexts which help to construct and inform them. As with all personal experience methodologies, it is for individual readers to bring their own experiences to the retelling of the stories.

The book will inevitably be a 'messy text' because the stories are ongoing and changes are still happening in our lives. The stories we tell today may not be the ones we would tell tomorrow as we continually struggle to make sense of our assumptions, experiences and lives. In striving to do this, we have drawn on feminism, intersectionality, personal experience approaches to research amongst other things, to illuminate some of these assumptions. As Bartky writes:

> coming to have a feminist conscience is the experience of coming to see things about oneself and one's society that were heretofore hidden. ...The scales fall from our eyes. We begin to understand why we have such depreciated images of ourselves ... Understanding, even beginning to understand this, makes it possible to change. Coming to see things differently, we are able to make out possibilities for liberating collective action and for unprecedented personal growth ... Moreover that feeling of alienation from established society which is so prominent a feature of feminist experience may be counter-balanced by a new identification with women of all conditions and a growing sense of solidarity with other feminists. (Bartky, 1990:21)

Yet while we have found placing our own personal struggles into the public domain challenging, it is also enabling, for it confirms in all of us the importance of uncertainty, of 'not knowing' but instead 'searching for' and of the need for humility in the process. When we first met to share our initial thoughts, fears and concerns, we asked each other for complete honesty when reading and responding to our drafts. It is not easy to tell one's story – especially once it has been acknowledged that the very process of the production, let alone the text itself, is partial, ongoing, subject to change, challenge and scrutiny by others. As supervisors, we remind students that the doctoral thesis can never be complete, never perfect, never 'done' – as Helen notes – but will be returned to and 'dusted off' from time to time. If, as Bartky notes above, as a result of writing this book, we as authors and you as readers come to see any part of our lives differently, and we can challenge further our assumptions and certainties, then we believe the book will have been a success.

In offering these narratives we aimed to open up the possibility of constructing 'a different relationship between the researchers and subjects and between authors and readers' (Ellis and Bochner, 2000: 744). We wanted to present, as Art Bochner did, 'a more personal, collaborative, and interactive relationship, one that centered on the question of how human experience is endowed with meaning and on the moral and ethical choices we face as human beings who live in an uncertain and changing world' (Ellis and Bochner, 2000:744).

This book is about how women's lives can be and have been changed through and by academic study for a higher research degree. But it is also about how past and present social and political changes influence these lives. It is about complexity, contradictions and tensions; the opening up and closing down of aspirations, opportunities and experiences, some taken, some achieved, some missed. It is about the creation of opportunities by others in the past for their daughters' daughters in the future. It is about how we are creating possibilities for our own daughters and their daughters in the future. It is also about the way in which different contexts, historical, political and sociological, all play their part in this creation of opportunity and complexity.

All the chapters have an underlying feminist principle: the belief that the 'personal is political'. Chapter 2, *Accessing Doctoral Education: processes of becoming an academic*, highlights the significance of this. Penny Jane Burke's narrative locates her own process of becoming an academic within the context of widening participation in higher education and her own insights and struggles around issues of access and participation. She examines the 'gendered experiences of doing a PhD and the way this shapes the multiple and contradictory constructions of an academic subjectivity'. Penny positions herself within the two 'greedy' institutions of higher education and family and discusses the sometimes 'painful and troublesome' demands and expectations made by both of them, likening herself to a 'time and space traveller' whose different worlds are sometimes in collision. But at the same time she is able to draw on transferable skills from both spheres. Her chapter also makes clear the non-linearity, complexity and contradictory nature of any journey into academia.

Chapter 3 offers Barbara Ann Cole's narrative, '*Good' vibrations: good girls, good wives, good mothers and good heavens – a PhD*. In it she considers her own somewhat accidental journey into academic life and her involvement in the field of inclusive education. She highlights the uncertainties, complexities and contradictions of bringing together rhetoric and reality, principle and practice and the inevitable personal and professional negotiations involved as a mother and teacher in a context where difference can be perceived as deviance; and where powerful discourses constructed professionals as experts, and mothers on different sides of the binary divide between the powerful public and the invisible private. Challenging this divide through her own doctoral study encouraged Barbara to explore and be comfortable with uncertainty, and to challenge perceived givens.

Gloria Gordon contributes her narrative in Chapter 4, *Researching Life Itself: human centred passionate appreciation*. She draws on her experiences as a black women and mother on the 'periphery of British society in an insider/outside position'. Silencing, race, negative labelling, powerful emotional backlash and low self esteem all emerge in Gloria's account as she examines the contradictions between 'what is espoused publicly and what actually happens where race is concerned as a social issue'. Gloria believes that if she had not adopted a practitioner/researcher approach she would not have completed her doctoral studies. She reflects on her self-reconstruction, the impact of her own work in the field and the particular contribution she has made in de-constructing 'black socialisation', and the positioning of the black community in British society. Gloria's chapter highlights the importance of self-knowledge, not as a 'self indulgent or narcissistic pursuit', but rather as 'essential to dispelling the illusions and confusions which we all learn and which lead us down wrong paths'. Her story clearly illustrates that her 'educational ideas did not develop through academic efforts made in the quiet and relative leisure of the study. Rather they were born of the back-and-forth interplay between theory and practice under a multitude of pressures'.

Chapter 5, *Dusting off my Doctorate*, presents Helen Gunter's account of her journey into academia. The chapter opens with Helen's reflections on her thesis as 'not only an account of something that I spent five years of my life thinking and writing about, but also there is a history here of my life'. Yet the thesis is 'no autobiographical revelation of who I am or why I am as I am, but is instead a narrative about dust that, in looking back from now, means something about how I understood then'. Helen's narrative is far from linear and takes the reader through her exploration of 'rational' libraries and the works she found there written by people 'older, wiser, normally male and more powerful than me ... and they were often dead so I had to respect their lives and work'. From this she came to realise that her own field of educational management had not been studied or examined. Reflecting back to her time as a secondary school teacher, she questioned the origins of the rapidly growing field of educational management in the 1990s following the 1988 Education Reform Act. Through her academic studies, Helen found her place among what she refers to as the 'dusty shelves'. Yet Helen's story also explores the intersections of class, education, gender, culture and higher education. Again, the importance of silence as an 'appropriate' response is an emerging theme. Working class northern girls did not challenge professors! Helen explores how comprehensive education, a first degree and then a PhD (and Bourdieu) helped her to reconstruct her own identity, particularly as a writer challenging 'how to do it' ringbinders".

Jennifer Lavia, in her chapter, *Teachers, Postcoloniality and the PhD*, seeks to reconceptualise how context, culture, positionality, and other social phenomena can impact on experience. Central to her chapter is the importance of writing as a black Caribbean woman 'involved in innovative teacher education programmes conducted in the Caribbean by a British University'. So issues of race, class, gender and identity 'become central points of interrogating historical, colonial centre-periphery relations'. This chapter too points to contradictions of 'knowledge, place, context and belonging' and once again, Jennifer points to the importance of having been party to 'theory in practice'. Her account tells of the political and educational struggle to set up a teachers' professional development programme from the 'bottom up, largely unrecognised by the Academy and having to create its own ways of being and doing as we went'. From this emerged Jennifer's own PhD, as she set out to examine teacher development in Trinidad and Tobago, drawing on post-colonial analysis. Jennifer reflects on the personal cost; the missed family events and opportunities with her son, the mornings waking up at the computer with her son asleep on her lap. Again the response of silence. Emerging from her story is the importance of her own early biographical reflections which led her to want to explore the relationship between 'teachers and a politics of change'. She draws on the work of Freire to explore how her own 'history, work, culture and values [were] shaped by the experience of being and 'living in the field' were to be recognised in the critical authorship of the study'.

The last narrative comes from Heidi Safia Mirza, writing with Kate Hoskins. Chapter 7 *Love in the Cupboard: A conversation about success and sadness when race, gender and class collide in the making of an academic career*, offers a different format. Heidi's chapter is in the form of an autobiographical conversation with Kate, in which she tells of her journey into academia and how she came to do a PhD. As with Gloria and Jennifer, the intersections of race, gender, feminism and culture are brought together amidst the incompleteness, complexities and contradictions of reflexive autobiographical accounts. Heidi's account is different in that is also offers direct insight into the impact of offering such narratives to those currently undertaking a PhD. Kate, as interviewer, finds that the interview is 'nourishing' her own PhD. It also offers insights into some of the methodological issues, noted earlier, of using narratives in social science research. The title of Heidi's chapter relates to her mother being hidden in the cupboard when her husband's family came to visit. In this account the issue to be hidden is her mother's whiteness, but in many ways it could act as a metaphor in each of the stories, because within each is something hidden or kept silent. Heidi's recognition that her PhD was a pivotal moment is common to all the narratives for, through it, silences were ultimately broken.

The last chapter, *Beginings and Ends*, opens with the wonderful and oh so relevant poem by Karin Oerlemans (2007), which not one of us would contradict a single word of; take note those who have not yet begun your doctoral journeys. The editors look back on the narratives as a whole and draw out some of the connections, continuities, discontinuities and contradictions, changes or transformations.

While we offer the narratives here as possibly less eloquent and poetic accounts of our own doctoral journeys, we remind ourselves that they are only partial accounts, only ever, as Kate Hoskins notes, the stories we may or may not tell on a good or bad day. They are not offered as accounts of 'how it was for us', intended to encourage or deter readers from embarking on or continuing doctoral research. Rather, we ask you to read them and relate to them from and through your own intersections, perspectives, contradictions etc. You may ask yourself whether these accounts are 'true' and how you should evaluate them. These are difficult questions for the researcher using personal experience methodologies. And our reply is to respond with uncertainty, hopefully with humility and to return a question to you in the hesitant, uncertain but ultimately comforting words of Sandelowski:

When you talk with me about my research, do not ask me what I found; I found nothing. Ask me what I invented, what I made up from and out of my data. But know that in asking you to ask me this, I am not confessing to telling any lies about the people or events in my studies/stories. I have told the truth. The proof for you is in the things I have made – how they look to your mind's eye, whether they satisfy your sense of style and craftsmanship, whether you believe them, and whether they appeal to your heart. (Sandelowski, 1994:61)

2

Accessing Doctoral Education: processes of becoming an academic

Penny Jane Burke

Introduction

Widening participation in higher education is a central policy theme and has received vast attention ranging from government policy, politicians and public speakers, to the media and researchers. The New Labour government invested a great deal of funding and resources into the effort to reach those who are under-represented in higher education, and universities have appointed staff with specific responsibility for widening participation (WP). Developing activities such as summer schools, road shows and workshops has been a major strand of WP strategy, informed by the concern to raise the aspirations of potential students from disadvantaged backgrounds. Students from such backgrounds have been recruited in their universities to act as mentors and ambassadors to encourage other such candidates and to show that with determination, disadvantaged individuals with potential can succeed. A meritocratic view of education is re-established through these strategies, interventions and approaches.

In many ways I am the ideal subject of widening participation policy and have been constructed in various contexts as a positive role model for other women. In this chapter, I deconstruct the contested meanings that circulate around the processes of being positioned as a subject of WP policy and the implications of this for subjective construction. I trace my journey through my experiences as a mature non-traditional student from Access to PhD student, theorising my account by drawing on feminist post-structural perspectives. I draw on my 'memory work' (Giroux, 1998) to reconstruct my experiences of being a student-subject, locating my memories in particular social, political and cultural contexts and relations. I reconstruct my memory work in relation to key policy discourses and to significant discourses around gendered and academic subjectivities. The chapter seeks to draw on my personal experiences as a case study, to tease out and critique the problematic discourses that are at play within educational and policy contexts about students from non-traditional backgrounds. Such discourses continue to shape my sense of subjectivity and the ways I negotiate my contradictory positionings within the micro-politics of academic life.

This chapter first presents the theoretical framework for the analysis of my memories and re-constructions and sets the policy background. My memory work follows – an analytical discussion pulling out key themes and issues which illuminate the challenges of accessing doctoral studies as a mature non-traditional student. Insights of feminist post-structural perspectives are drawn upon to highlight the struggles around access and participation, the gendered experiences of doing a PhD and how this shapes the multiple and contradictory constructions of an academic subjectivity.

Policy context

I first accessed education through an Access to Higher Education course in North-East London in the early 1990s. It was the year before polytechnics were assigned university status and Access courses still had the explicitly politicised profile first established in the late 1970s and early 1980s, with a deep concern to redress social inequalities by transforming education to challenge elitism and inequality. 'The access movement [drew] upon a radical approach to education which asks for a fundamental shift in the distribution of cultural capital' (Williams, 1997:43). At this political moment, the access movement was driven by the perspectives of practitioners, located outside central state sponsorship and thus relatively free from the tight regulation imposed on Access courses today. The needs of students and local communities were placed as a central concern in the design of courses and curricula (Diamond, 1999:186).

However, this is only one dimension of the access movement. It was heterogeneous across localised contexts and the practices across and within different Access courses varied widely. On the Access course I took, practices were mixed: in some ways the course was radical in approach, because it explicitly articulated a political stance by critiquing the educational system. This was seen as exclusive, reproductive of wider social inequalities and as working mainly in the interests of privileged groups. Yet simultaneously, the pedagogical approaches adopted were often embedded in traditional, didactic relations, with the teachers giving lectures positioned as the keepers of knowledge, and the students passively taking notes.

Over the 1990s there were significant cultural and managerial changes to Access courses as a result of its formalisation and national recognition. 'The incorporation of Access policy-makers into the decision-making processes of the dominant agencies' significantly reshaped Access developments (Diamond, 1999:184). The arrival of the national kitemark and the consequent legitimisation of Access courses resulted in 'a mass explosion of Access courses' (Diamond, 1999:186). As decision-making shifted from Access practitioners working within localised sites to policy-makers working at a national level, the underpinning concerns and values also shifted, away from social justice and towards the establishment of 'frameworks and structures to give legitimacy to the outcome of a student successfully completing an Access programme' (Diamond, 1999:185). The result was a shift from creating locally relevant courses to developing regulative systems of administration and organisation.

In mapping out the changing terrain of Access, then, it is important to note the different and competing discourses at play (1997: 42). Different social players, including politicians, access practitioners, educational managers and access students, have struggled to redefine, control and manage the access education agenda. In 1997, when New Labour came to power and declared access and participation to be a central theme of educational policy, 'widening participation' as a discourse gained momentum and hegemony. WP is a highly contested field, with different meanings attached to 'access' and 'WP'. It now developed into an agenda largely driven by economic and utilitarian concerns, such as skills development and employability.

In current policy and practice frameworks WP strategies tend to place emphasis on changing individual attitudes and are embedded in deficit constructions of individual lack (Jones and Thomas, 2005). Yet one should not oversimplify the unpredictable ways in which policy gets enacted and produced within localised sites, as these are always shaped by complex sets of micro-politics and relations of power (Ball, 1987; 1990; Morley, 1999). WP is discursively produced within specific political contexts, which means it is tied to competing sets of understanding about what higher education is for and for whom. There are, though, particular strands of hegemonic discourses that have prevailed and gained momentum over the past two decades, underpinned by neoliberalism, resulting in an overemphasis on individualism, business-oriented aspirations and the power of markets for education.

The HEFCE-funded organisation, Action on Access, explains the guidance provided on who should be targeted in relation to WP policy:

> The targeting guidance states that, as a principle, resources should be targeted at learners with the potential to benefit from higher education who come from under-represented communities. Overwhelmingly these learners are from lower socio-economic groups (groups 4-8 in the National Statistics Socio-economic Classification, NS-SEC) and those from disadvantaged backgrounds who live in areas of relative deprivation where participation in HE is low. (Action on Access, 2008)

WP policy discourse identifies individuals who are disadvantaged but have the potential to benefit from higher education (HE). WP discourse is thus inextricably tied to the politics of identity and inequalities of class, ethnicity, gender and race, as well as other differences. As Archer points out, competing discourses of class, gender and race

> ... that prevail within educational policy at any particular time will directly influence and shape the forms of practice that are subsequently undertaken within schools', colleges and universities. (Archer, 2003:21).

The taken-for-granted acceptance that the economy and marketplace are at the centre of the project to widen participation implicates different individuals and communities in differing ways, contributing to hierarchies of difference and processes of the subjective construction of the university student. This acceptance is shaped by the discourses of neoliberalism in which 'equality of opportunity [is] recast as the individualising of opportunities, for economic and social enhancement' (Arnot *et al*, 1999:83).

Neoliberalism directs policy attention to individual aspirations and foregrounds individual responsibility, self-determination and employability in the context of uncertain, unstable and fluctuating market forces (Archer *et al*, 2003; Blackmore, 2006; Brine, 2006; Burke and Jackson, 2007; Clegg and David, 2006; Morley, 2003; Reay *et al*, 2001). Although the emphasis is on self-improvement within what is constructed as a meritocratic system, policy also makes reference to the importance of social justice, which is expressed through the discourse of inclusion. This discourse helps challenge policy that focuses too heavily on *increasing* participation rather than *widening* it to tackle social exclusion. The discourse of inclusion is also problematic, however, as it aims to 'include those who are excluded into the dominant framework/ state of being, rather than challenging existing inequalities within the mainstream system, or encouraging alternative ways of being' (Archer, 2003:23).

The discourse of inclusion constructs a diverse British society constituted of individual citizens who, regardless of their social position and background, share universal values and perspectives. The implication is that all British citizens must aspire to be included in a set of shared orientations, ignoring that these tend to privilege middleclassed, white racialised, ablest and heterosexist subject positions. Differences associated with marginality, disadvantage and deficit must thus be regulated and controlled. Although 'diversity' is celebrated, and used by universities to promote their profile, being 'too different' requires self-correction and self-regulation.

Finally, and importantly for this chapter, WP policy has been largely concerned with undergraduate level study. Postgraduate study is often seen as beyond the concerns of WP policy and practice. This is partly due to notions of 'standards' and 'quality' and the privileging of the 'academic' at postgraduate level. In policy documents and media coverage, WP has been continually juxtaposed with anxieties about lowering standards. Hence, a key strategy of WP has been to create new forms of higher education. In England this has largely been the creation of two-year, work-based Foundation degrees. Masters degrees and doctoral prgrammes are safeguarded as primarily academic spaces (although there are professional postgraduate courses, such as EdD) where concerns about WP are seen as less relevant. Additionally, there is an assumption that the 'WP student' becomes transformed through the process of participating in undergraduate level courses into a different kind of subject and participant. By the time the WP student graduates with a BA honours degree, it is assumed that she will be reconstituted as 'the same' as the traditional honours degree student. It has been argued that WP is about changing working-class individuals into middle-class subjects (Archer and Leathwood, 2003) and this upholds the view that access to postgraduate level study is irrelevant to the WP project.

Theorising Access to Higher Education

I have drawn on feminist post-structuralism to shed light on my experiences and the wider processes of subjective construction in relation to accessing higher education. Feminist post-structural perspectives provide the conceptual tools to deconstruct the problematic assumptions underpinning the deficit constructions of the 'WP student' and to expose the ways such constructions might reinforce rather than destabilise complex operations of exclusions and inequality across educational sites and relations. This approach illuminates the significance of subjective construction and subjectification in struggles over access to and participation in higher education and postgraduate level study. It is illuminating to examine the discursive processes of exclusions and mis/recognition, by interrogating how subjects become recognisable as students within regulatory and disciplinary institutional spaces. Feminism helps to focus on structural inequalities and unequal power relations, in relation to gender and other sets of intersecting differences, whilst post-structuralism helps shed light on the ways subjects are constituted through discourses.

In analysing my memory work and the reconstructions of my experiences written for this chapter, I draw on Butler's concept of subjectification (1997). The concept is useful in deconstructing the WP subject position, as it emphasises subjectivity as productive, constituted

24

through discourse, and tied to the complex processes of inclusion and recognition. Davies explains:

> Central to the dual process of submission and mastery in the formation of the subject are the mutual acts of recognition through which subjects accord each other the status of viable subjecthood. (Davies, 2006:427)

WP policy and practice is implicated in the dual processes of submission and mastery in the formation and recognition of the WP subject. WP is something that is done to and for those from under-represented and disadvantaged groups by means of WP 'activities'. The discourse neatly encompasses those recognised as 'WP students' as 'under-represented' and 'disadvantaged' (see for example, HEFCE, 2006), subjecting them to the 'disciplinary gaze' (Foucault, 1984) of WP policy discourse. To be re-cognisable as a subject of this policy, the person must be subjected to the discourses of disadvantage, re/positioning the WP subject as the dif-ferent and 'Other' of educational policy, yet actively engaged in a project of self-improvement through educational participation, mastering the skills needed to succeed (see for example, DfEE, 1999). Subjective forma-tion is always constructed through difference, in relation to what is con-structed as the 'Other' (Hall, 2000:17). Student subjectivities are con-structed through difference and 'polarising discourses' and are tied to the notion of an ideal-student subject; the traditional, standard, 18 year old student (Williams, 1997:26). Those students associated with WP must overcome the demeaning subject position of the disadvantaged.

> The normal, the worthy student and the acceptable processes of admission are legitimised by references to the abnormal, the unworthy the unaccept-able. (Williams, 1997:25 cited in Burke, 2002)

In this chapter, I draw on feminist post-structural concepts of subjec-tivity to examine and interrogate my memory work in relation to pro-cesses of inclusion and exclusion in the doctoral programme and later in becoming an academic. I consider this in relation to my educational memories, experiences and aspirations in light of my struggles for re-cognition as a worthy subject of and in higher education. Subjective construction is a destabilising project of 'becoming' and 'doing' rather than 'being'. Subjectivity highlights the relational processes of identity formations and focuses on the ways people 'are both 'made subject' by/within the social order and how they are agents/subjects within/

against it' (Jones, 1993:158). Subjects move across and between fluid and contradictory positions, and are subjected to, as well as resistors of, the competing discourses at play (Davies, 1997:275).

The discursive constitution of subjectivities is located within debates and policies that generate particular understandings of WP. Hegemonic discourses of WP constrain and make possible competing understandings of what it means to be a university student as well as to profoundly shape educational policies and practices (Burke and Jackson, 2007: 112). As Hall observes, 'identities are constructed through, not outside, difference' (Hall, 2000:17).

Accessing education: becoming a student

My discovery of Access to Higher Education was entirely serendipitous. At the time, I was newly married, and had the full-time responsibility of caring for my three-year-old son and seven-year-old stepson. It was the early 1990s. I had recently survived a traumatic experience of domestic violence and had lived for a time in a women's aid refuge. The experiences of violence and of escaping and surviving altered my world perspectives profoundly. Although I always cared about social justice, I did not understand why, nor did I have an articulate or explicit sense of the politics of social justice.

My traumatic experiences politicised me and I wanted to seek answers and, like many others, I wanted to find a way to 'give back'. This sense of purpose and urgency was partly connected to the identity project of redefining a legitimate subjecthood, as I often described myself as 'rebuilding my life'. Before the domestic abuse I was completely submerged and invested in becoming a ballerina, and this powerfully defined my sensibilities as a gendered subject. I constituted myself through the discourses of femininity, drawing on particularly delicate and 'ladylike' subject positions, my sense of self strongly formed through the Hollywood glamour and the fairy-like ballet world I grew up in. My subject position as an included and recognised subject revolved around the recognition of being a 'lady' and being seen as demure and elegant. The loss of the availability of the ballerina subject position, which came together with leaving behind home during my period of escape, followed by the kindness and support of those working for women's aid, fuelled a strong desire to 'give back' in some way.

The women's aid refuge was managed in a feminist way; it was my first explicit experience of feminism and feminist politics. As I focused on the project of rebuilding my life, I wanted to understand my experience better. Although I had no grand plan and no access to the discursive or material resources to develop this understanding, I had desire and determination. I started to meet women who did have access to the cultural and discursive practices required to re/formulate a subject positioning from feminine to feminist. One woman told me about a local Access to Higher Education course and an open evening. I attended this: the moment was significant and stands out as inspiring. I immediately decided that I would take the course and become a primary school teacher.

The bus ride back home was a blur of adrenalin and excitement as a sense of anticipation and possibility surged through my body. Here was a chance! An opportunity! My son could go to nursery at the College while I studied to become a teacher. I imagined myself in a classroom at a blackboard, with a room full of sweet children in front of me. The joy! Everything would be ok.

Becoming a teacher felt possible and realistic. I had my own children and I had taught ballet to children in my previous life (pre-domestic violence was experienced as the 'before' and I was now in the 'after'). Teaching primary school was constructed as a natural extension of my existing sense of self as mother and dance teacher. The aspiration to become a schoolteacher did not disrupt my sensibilities; it felt familiar and comfortable. The Access course accommodated my material needs as a mother; the nursery was on campus, but also met my emotional need to be recognised as the aspirational, talented and successful subject. The refashioning of subjectivity was experienced as smooth and familiar; I felt a strong sense of belonging at the further education college where I studied. I had always been recognised as a 'good student', which fits in easily with being a 'feminine girl'. The move from budding ballerina to college student had a sense of continuity; one supported the other in a seamless move from being disciplined through the strict demands of ballet class to being disciplined through the intellectual rigour of academic study. I was the 'non-traditional', 'mature' Access student but I was in many ways the ideal-student subject. Once again in my life I was positioned as the recognised subject of potential and talent, of discipline and hard work. The cultural practices of the Access course fitted in well with those of the ballet world: it was all about listening, learning and reiterating the discursive practices of the teacher.

Becoming a university student

By the time I completed my Access course – and with Distinction – two days before giving birth to my youngest son, my subject positioning as the ambitious student had led me to desire something beyond primary school teaching. I decided to do a BA Honours degree, where I could pursue my new interest in Sociology rather than a BEd. Like most mature, non-traditional Access students, I did not consciously select a university to study at but went to the local post-1992 university, which had a compact agreement with the college where I had completed my Access course.

However, making the transition from college to university was not quite as comfortable and familiar as my previous transition into study. The university was big, intimidating and the practices were unfamiliar. Large lecture theatres were alienating places, and although I looked forward to the smaller seminar groups I was often terrified to speak out or contribute to the discussion in case I got it wrong and exposed myself as an illegitimate subject of WP policy.

Eventually though, I began to settle in as I negotiated the unfamiliar subject position of university student. Drawing again on the disciplinary practices of ballet, I soon learned how to fit in to the academic practices of the university and my confidence as a legitimate member of the student community began to rise. One memory stands out as important in the process of negotiating my subject positioning.

The tutor for my second year sociology module is awful. He rarely shows up to lectures and seminars and when he does, he passes out a handout and then tells us he has another meeting to attend. The group is made up of a lot of other mature women students, many of whom I have become friendly with. Last week, he deserted the class again and we have an exam next week. Most of the women are very anxious; they don't understand the material and think they will fail the exam. I have done the reading and I think I understand the sociological concepts and will do fine in the exam. I took a group of women together after class and gave them a tutorial to try to help them. I think they feel a lot better now.

As I began to reconstitute my subjectivity as a good student through mastering the academic practices and sociological concepts required, my subject positioning amongst the other mature women students began to change. I was recognised as the 'knowing subject' – the one who could provide help and support. As a familiar subject position, I embraced it and constructed myself as the 'teaching student' and this was strongly connected with a maternalistic, caring positioning. But this did not include the subject position as the academic or intellectual student; I was different and differentiated myself from the young students, whom I constructed as legitimate students. My success, on the other hand, I saw as purely through the virtue of drawing on the practices of ballet: working hard, immersing myself, listening, watching and reiterating the 'proper' practices of those who 'really know'. Thus I was positioned as Other in two ways: as the Other to the traditional university student, who came from an 'intellectual background' and 'really knew', and as the Other to the 'non-traditional' students who came from working-class backgrounds and had the potential to know. Although I mastered some of the requisite practices of the university, I also submitted to the position as Other and embraced my difference from the nomalised subject; the traditional 18-year old student who had completed A levels at Sixth Form. I saw my entitlement to be a student as provisional, conditional and unstable.

However, as a reflexive subject, dedicated to the project of understanding the nature of my experiences, I became increasingly interested in the connections between my personal experiences as a mature, woman, non-traditional student and the women I met along the way. I recognised the importance of gendered identity in all our daily negotiations. I was struck by the compelling and powerful stories these women told about their pain and struggle. They accessed higher education against the odds; they were like me. Both identification and disidentification were at play in the constitution of my subjectivity as a university student. Central to my recognition as a student with potential was my own story of survival, my ability to master the practices of the university and my passionate commitment to women's access to higher education. I was encouraged to follow through and develop my insights further and this led to my application for a Masters Degree in Women's Studies and Education.

Becoming a doctoral student

Once on the MA programme, I had access to a range of resources usually reserved for the privileged. The theoretical perspectives introduced on the course were challenging, frightening, exciting and demanding. A new world was opened to me; one in which women had struggled for equality and rights in ways I had not known about before. I felt I was an outsider and an intruder; I had no right to be on a course with women who had been political activists, who had a genuine entitlement to the honorary naming as feminist. My traumatic experiences gave me some sense of connection with wider feminist struggles but I felt naïve and ignorant in so many ways. There was so much to learn. I was determined to change myself for the better, to pour myself into the course and to make up for my apolitical disposition to the world in my previous life. I did have a specific sense of entitlement though; I was there for the rights of other women to access higher education.

The contradictions of this stance did not strike me until years later; my only way of understanding my entitlement to access the course was through repositioning myself in traditionally feminine ways – I was there to 'care' for the needs of others. Yet, I did have an in-depth under-standing of the complex issues involved in the experiences of accessing higher education from outsider subjective positionings and I could draw on these insights to develop a theoretical standpoint. The feminist writing I was introduced to was inspirational and in some ways familiar; it gave me the tools to articulate my experiences in ways that had not been available to me before.

My MA tutors were remarkable women in my view and I looked up to them to show me the way. Although I learned the importance of being critical, I was still the ballet student, following the fluid and elegant directions of my teachers, now through words, theories and concepts rather than movements and choreography. However, despite the em-phasis of ballet on the physical and academic study on the intellectual, I found the disciplinary processes astonishingly similar and was able to find spaces of inclusion and recognition in becoming a 'good' post-graduate student. My MA personal tutor took me under her wing and strongly encouraged me to pursue a PhD. I was thrilled to be identified as a potential doctoral student, although when I looked at the 'real' doctoral students around me, I had a strong sense of disidentification. I was nowhere near as intelligent as they were; I did not have the appropriate background and my knowledge was full of holes. I confided in my tutor and she reassured me that everyone had gaps in their knowledge. Drawing on feminist theory to support my self-belief, that knowledge is always tied to social relations and is always partial and in process, I decided that perhaps she was right. I struggled against the deficit discourses that not only framed my experiences but also shaped my self-understandings.

After completing my Masters, I registered on a part-time PhD and took on my first educational post. I was the Programme Manager of the Return to Study programme at a local further education college. My doctoral supervisor (who had been my MA tutor) encouraged me to apply for an ESRC studentship. I worked and reworked the application under her supervisory guidance, and was delighted when the ESRC informed me that I had been successful.

I'm sitting at my desk at work but I can't concentrate on work at all. I have asked the ESRC if I can change my request for a part-time studentship award to full-time. This way I can quit my job and focus full-time on my studies! I will continue to teach part-time for my ethnographic study but this would give me the freedom to focus completely on my research. I can't wait any more and pick up the phone to speak to the officer in charge of my award at the ESRC. My heart is beating fast as I ask her if a decision has been made. She says, so matter-of-factly, that certainly I can change from part-time to full-time status. I am bursting with excitement.

The ESRC studentship award validated my position and gave me legitimacy as a research student. These personal experiences and emotions illuminated the theoretical perspectives I was studying, for example about processes of marginalisation and misrecognition, and helped me to develop my approaches to understanding the mature women students in my study.

However, it was through the participation in a feminist poststructural reading group that I discovered an approach that could address the pains, dislocations and complexities of the experiences of accessing higher education from a non-traditional background. This was an important opportunity for me, particularly as a student with childcare responsibilities I rarely had the chance to discuss ideas with my peers and rushed in and out of the university for my supervisory meetings, just in time to make the school run. Time was precious and tightly regulated and had to fit in with the rhythm of family life, even though I was formally a full-time student. This meant having to work on my doctoral research mainly within school hours. The reading group offered me a space for intellectual discussion and support. As a feminist space, the pedagogy of the group insisted on creating a 'safe' and supportive space for the exploration of complex and difficult ideas. It felt collaborative rather than competitive, although there were also times when I felt anxious about speaking out in case I exposed myself as not really being intelligent after all.

Most importantly, it introduced me to a number of concepts that I had brushed by because I couldn't get my head around them on my own. The discussion in the reading group helped me to develop an understanding of these concepts and their significance for the analysis of my research data. Now I could expose the destabilising and unsettling experiences of accessing higher education, the complex operations of inequality, exclusion and misrecognition and the ways that students were subjected to the discourses at play within the social sites in which they were located (e.g. the college and the family). I was able to trace the processes of subjective construction in which they were constituted as mis/recognised subjects of widening participation policy. During this period, my analysis and writing developed significantly and I moved closer to producing a final version of my thesis.

Meanwhile, my supervisor met with the editor of Trentham Books for a project she was involved in and it emerged that Trentham was looking to publish a book on widening participation. I was asked to contact the editor and she requested that I send her a book proposal. My proposal was accepted and so I began the process of writing my thesis and book simultaneously.

This process was illuminating; it gave me insight into the writing practices attached to different forms of academic writing. For example, I was often told by the editor that my writing was 'too academic' and I needed to ensure it was written accessibly to a broad audience, which included policy-makers, educational managers, students as well as academics and researchers. I became interested in the connections between access, writing practices and epistemology (eg Burke and Hermer-schmidt, 2005; Burke, 2008). This helped me to understand that writing is not just a technique, which can be taught to access students as 'study skills', but was tied in with struggles over the construction of knowledge, voice and authority.

Becoming an academic

Women academics from working-class and minority ethnic back-grounds have written about their experiences of their changing and contradictory class positionings and the effects of this on emotions, subjectivity and relationships to others. Key themes emerging from this body of work are strong sensibilities of not belonging, of being the 'intruder' and of being 'caught out' (Reay, 1997; Clancy, 1997; Morley, 1997). These women scholars have expressed a feeling of being dis-covered to be a 'fraud'. This rests on feelings of never being good enough to be a legitimate academic (Stuart, 2000). These expressions of being outside the legitimate and acceptable forms of being an academic strongly resonate with my own sensibilities and subjective positionings. These lived experiences and academic writings are useful insights in developing a more nuanced understanding into the problematic ways WP subjects get positioned and position themselves within academic contexts.

These scholarly, personal and research-informed perspectives have led me to focus on subjective construction as a key concept in understand-ing the operations of inequality and misrecognition (Fraser, 1997) in higher education, which include the material and structural as well as the cultural and discursive (Burke, 2002; Burke and Jackson, 2007). The latter dimensions are particularly difficult to tease out in the everyday experiences of being a student or academic and expose the limitations of mainstream approaches to WP, which are concerned mainly with 'lifting barriers'. I have thus tried to show in my research that although concrete barriers such as travel, funding and childcare are significant, they are easier to identify and one can then develop policies accord-ingly. Furthermore, a focus primarily on barriers diverts attention from the work of uncovering the histories, complexities and depth of inequalities and misrecognitions at play in higher education. It is imperative to pay close attention to the ways in which misrecognitions and power relations are constructed, produced and reinforced within institutional spaces, not least because many institutional practices are re/productive of historical misrecognitions linked with age, class, disability, ethnicity, gender, nationality, race and sexuality (Burke and Jackson, 2007).

Ironically, such experiences have in many ways helped me to develop an academic career, because my (reconstructed and partial) story is recognised as helpful to other women and students from non-traditional backgrounds. In this way, I have often been institutionally positioned as a role model and have been identified as better able to relate to students, often by referring to my personal accounts of doing a PhD and becoming an academic. This has indeed formed an integral part of my teaching practices, largely shaped by feminist pedagogies that insist on the personal as a tool of critical learning. Furthermore, my story has been presented in various contexts as an alternative story of becoming an academic, which has been effective partly because it satisfies a political desire to create other possibilities for subjectivity within higher education, particularly in relation to the discourses of WP, individualism and self-determination.

Feminism has enabled me to negotiate inclusion within higher education – for example by citing feminist assertions that the personal is the political/theoretical and that personal experiences illuminate important processes, experiences and conceptual themes. This allows me to show how my story is also your story and our story because subjectivities are always constituted through discourse and social relations of power and difference. The insistence on drawing on personal reflection to make sense of social and critical theory is an important dimension of feminist pedagogy that I have applied in my teaching as well as in my research, writing and educational management. Feminist pedagogies have thus offered me different ways of being an academic that are available and possible, even desirable, because of the political struggles of my 'fore mothers': those who have actively struggled for women's rights, women's ways of being and women's ways of knowing.

However, feminist post-structuralism and other bodies of feminist theory, such as Black feminism, have challenged some of the related feminist assumptions as problematically rooted in essentialist notions which reinforce gendered subjectivities rather than destabilise them. These competing theories have been central in my personal negotiation of becoming an academic, underpinned by the principles of feminism as a politicised positioning within higher education. I am both struggling for the recognition of feminised ways of knowing and participating in projects that aim to deconstruct and challenge problematic gendered subjectivities.

Although I have embraced poststructuralism as offering a range of conceptual tools to understand the complexity of formations of subjectivity, feminism has also offered me a reconfigured positioning as woman. This requires attention to structures, power relations and differences, which are not quite as fluid as poststructural theorists might claim them to be. Feminism aims to understand the ways in which women and men are gendered subjects, negotiating formations of femininities and masculinities across complex power relations, and to theorise the ways in which experiences and knowledge are also gendered. Yet, poststructuralism aims to destabilse the subject, deconstructing humanist understandings of identity as stable and reconceptualising identities as always constituted through discourse. In these ways, as I have considered in previous work (Burke, 2002), feminism and poststructuralism are discordant theoretical perspectives. However, like many other feminists, I believe the conceptual tools of poststructuralism are valuable in deconstructing processes of gendered subjectivity, in understanding the subject as formed through doing as well as being and as theorising the subject of gendered discourse as always in process and thus open to transformative ways of being. The insights of feminist poststructuralism have been helpful to me, not only in negotiating my work as a researcher and teacher, but also in other responsibilities as an academic, including being head of school.

Feminist poststructuralism has helped me to analyse and critically consider the contradictory positions and discourses I engage in as a woman academic. For example, one of the arguments I have made in my work on widening participation is that it is underpinned by neo-liberalism, which implicates different subjects of WP in processes of self-discipline and self-regulation (eg Burke, 2006, 2008, 2009). WP policy is a form of disciplinary technology that requires subjects to seek continually to improve themselves through neoliberal discourses of flexibility, adaptability and self-determination and against the measure of the normalised subject. The irony of my own relation to such discourses has not passed me by; as I write about the problematic of such regulatory discourses I am implicated in them as I struggle to be recognised as a legitimate academic subject. This has entailed embracing the demands of neoliberal discourses in higher education that require academics to be flexible, whilst simultaneously developing a specialism and area of expertise.

The legitimate academic of the early twenty-first century in Britain must produce work that is seen as 'world-class', as regulated by the Research Assessment Exercise (soon to be the Research Excellence Framework), must meet the expectations of excellence in quality assurance systems on teaching and learning and must demonstrate the skills to manage and lead academic work. Yet at the same time, the academic must also be able to teach in new areas according to the changing student and employment markets, must be able to bid successfully for research funding in an increasingly competitive and restrictive economically-oriented framework, and must be able to take on new challenges in a continual project of self-improvement and development.

In many ways, I am the 'ideal' neo-liberal subject. After completing my PhD, I took up a number of significant challenges, remaking myself and my expertise according to the needs of the institution and the market. The levels of flexibility I showed and my willingness to take up new challenges were rewarded with yet more challenges and the connected promotional opportunities tied to successfully undertaking these. However, the pains and struggles hidden by my performance as a self-determining and responsible subject, have been absorbed within my personal experiences, my health and well-being, as many other academic women experience in juggling multiple and conflicting demands. One of the significant responsibilities I agreed to undertake was the role of head of school.

As my colleagues congratulated me on my new role as Head of School, I smiled calmly, thanking them for their support. Inside my heart was throbbing and my tummy was full of butterflies; how did others have such confidence in me? Would I be able to do this job? The responsibility felt huge and I was terrified.

An important critique of feminist work on women's labour in higher education is to expose the gendered effects of femininity on women academic's experiences and dispositions to their work. This often involves taking on the emotional dimensions of academic work, particularly in terms of their pedagogical relations, with students as well as their colleagues. Women constitute only about 17 per cent of Heads of Department and Professors (ECU, 2009) largely because of the gendered division of labour in higher education and the family, both characterised by feminist scholars as 'greedy institutions' (Edwards, 1993). Women tend to take on more teaching, and when they do, they often spend more time on the caring and emotional aspects of the teacher-student relationship. Women are often in part-time temporary positions, making it more difficult to contribute to the other aspects of academic work, such as research and publication, which are privileged in universities and in promotion processes. Women often find it more difficult to take an individualist and competitive approach to their work, approaches which are most often rewarded in universities.

This is of course not to argue that many men don't also take collaborative approaches to their work and that many women are competitive and operate in individualist ways. However, formations of femininity make it more difficult for women to take up these ways of working, and women are more likely to be seen as 'a problem' and criticised when they do, because of hegemonic versions of doing woman. Thus the production of gendered subjectivities within institutions such as universities makes it more difficult for individual women to privilege research over teaching, in a wider framework where research is still seen as more important than teaching, particularly in higher-status institutions.

In my personal experiences, this has translated into taking on multiple responsibilities whilst making sure that I maintain my position as an active researcher, producing books and articles and bidding for research funding. I have had the opportunity to learn from inspiring mentors, who have encouraged and supported me. Their confidence in me has been key in my decisions to take on challenges I might have been too fearful to accept without their support and encouragement. Recognition is a powerful concept in illuminating my personal experiences of becoming an academic; legitimate others have recognised me as a legitimate subject. Without those processes of recognition, I would not have been included and constituted as an academic. Yet I also identify strongly with the women writing about their experiences of moving from working-class to academic subjectivities discussed above. My academic subjectivity is always in question, always on the edge, always full of uncertainty and self-questioning.

Being an academic has also been a complicated subjectivity to constitute alongside my subjectivity as wife and mother. Edwards (1993) named higher education and family as two greedy institutions and I have indeed found it painful and troublesome to negotiate the demands and expectations of both. Yet I have also desired both: wanting to be a successful academic and a good wife and mother. I have felt like a time and space traveller as I move between and across these spaces and moments in two worlds that often seemed to be in collision and sometimes in parallel. Moving across and between the competing demands of higher education and home (formed through institutional structures and discourses and through processes of self-discipline and regulation) created a sense of discontinuous, fragmented and unstable subject positions.

Yet simultaneously, in the neoliberal world I inhabit, where 'transferable skills' are valued and recognised, I have also been able to draw on being a mother to inform my pedagogical and research practices and to draw on my theoretical engagements with feminism to shape practices of mothering. In these ways the two institutions were co-supportive and complementary worlds, which eased processes of subjective construction and recognition. Furthermore, as feminist theory instructs us, I was significantly privileged by my positioning as a heterosexual, able-bodied, white, married woman with children, constructing me in normalised ways and giving me a legitimate narrative in which to explain my difficulties and struggles.

Conclusion

In this chapter, I have examined my reconstructed memories to demonstrate the sophisticated ways in which feminist poststructural theories uncover processes of inclusion and exclusion in higher education. I have examined this in relation to the policy of widening participation and my personal experiences of accessing higher education and becoming an academic through doctoral studies. In tracing the changing political perspectives of access and widening participation, I have situated my story in relation to wider social relations, policy discourses and processes of inclusion and recognition.

The feminist assertion that the personal is the political remains significant in theorising processes of subjective construction, as well as in developing inclusive practices in higher education, including pedagogical and leadership practices. My story highlights the way personal stories help to uncover complex struggles for recognition in higher education, challenging neoliberal accounts, which focus on individual determination and success. The operations of inequality at play within universities are highly complex and difficult to capture. The discourses of barriers cannot adequately address processes of exclusion and misrecognition. Accessing doctoral level study was central in gaining access to the political, theoretical and epistemological perspectives that have helped me negotiate an academic subject positioning and also to develop work on gendered experiences and subjectivities in relation to widening participation.

I have deconstructed my own positions and subjectivities in the processes and practices I engaged in and experienced as a WP student and in 'becoming' an academic. I have argued for the fragility of the project of recognition as a legitimate subject of higher education, even as I enjoyed the privileges of a white racialised and heterosexualised subjectivity and benefitted from the support of encouraging mentors. Accessing higher education at all degree levels, and becoming an academic, is not a simple, straightforward and linear journey of self-determination and progress, as neoliberal discourses might suggest. It is fraught with contradictions, emotional struggles and problematic assumptions, which create challenges of submission, resistance and mastery in becoming a recognisable subject within the gendered, classed and racialised spaces of higher educational institutions.

3

'Good' vibrations: good girls, good wives, good mothers and ... good heavens – a PhD?

Barbara Ann Cole

Having children changes your life (Sikes, 1997). On reflection the births of my two children, whilst very different, were for me the most wonderful, traumatic, confusing and disturbing experiences. With the birth of my daughter, my first born, the world became a different place and 'I' a different person within it. The perceived stability surrounding the roles in my life as daughter, woman, wife, lecturer and friend were totally upturned by the birth, after a month in hospital, of my daughter. This tiny baby proceeded to dominate my life for the next twenty two months. Relationships with 'others' were filtered through a lens of infant needs and demands. Only in relation to these did I consider my own identity, if I considered it at all through a haze of lost sleep, little food and snatched conversations. (Cole, 2002:9)

These are the opening lines of my doctoral thesis. I sometimes use them as an introduction to the narrative sessions I do with doctoral students. They are often surprised and sometimes shocked that I should begin an academic piece of work for examination and entry into the academy with such personal (and motherly) insights. I usually read two more pages, and they are even more surprised and even shocked that in those pages I briefly describe the illness which struck my son when he was only thirteen months old:

On a Sunday morning in November we found my son in his cot, deep in a coma. He was twitching slightly but there was no other response. He was thirteen months old. He had not been ill; he had shown no signs of anything which might suggest that there was a problem. Over the next few days he remained unconscious and still, except for the strange and disturbing fits which periodically twitched his strong little body. He had suffered a brain haemorrhage but the cause has never really been satisfactorily explained. It seems possible that he had an infantile stroke. (Cole, 2002:10)

These first few pages of the thesis are probably the most difficult words I have ever written. My son is now a man of thirty, married and living independently and the thesis is not located in a tragedy model of disability. This was part of my life, my son's life and my family's lives and they were going to be examined by others to determine if my work was 'good' enough to allow me access to the academy. My thesis explored the lived experiences of women who were mothers of children perceived as having special educational needs, but who were also teachers in the field of special education. I was a mother-teacher of a son perceived as having special educational needs, and it was my own personal and professional experiences which ultimately informed and underpinned my study. I wanted to know, 'whether there were other women who had similar experiences and if there were, what insights our lives might offer' (Cole, 2002:11).

These personal experiences were not left to stand alone, however. I contextualised the account within past and current social and educational policies (eg the Warnock Report, DES, 1978; the 1981 Education Act, DES, 1981; and the Education Reform Act DES, 1988), which in many ways influenced the personal and professional choices I made. In the following chapters I explored different 'ways of knowing' and the power of discourses to construct and 'other'. I drew on auto/biographical, narrative and personal experience methods literature as a counter to dominant discourses and to support my methodological approach. I presented the life stories of six other mother-teachers as individual accounts, contextualised against the background outlined above. I argued that my analysis was both embedded and embodied in the stories, in the data I had selected from the in-depth interviews and that it was illuminated through their historical, sociological and policy contextualisation.

While such an approach undoubtedly has its critics, I felt it was central to my thesis. My personal and professional experiences had collided and through the PhD I was able to reflect on these through different lenses. I did not seek objectivity, reliability, validity nor was I an unbiased researcher. I had positionality which I made clear within the thesis. I cared about the issues; not about what was right or wrong, for the stories suggested that there were multiple perspectives, complexities, contradictions and tensions, but about the importance of different voices being heard, rather than those of policy makers, 'experts' and the media.

The more I researched the context in which my own personal experiences and those of other women were located, the more I felt that these experiences mattered and could and should offer insights into what it meant and how it felt to live and to engage with policy in practice; to struggle with and between conflicting policies and dominant discourses which positioned women as 'unrealistic' mothers. Through my PhD studies and the work of feminists such as Smith, Oakley, David, Sawicki, and postmodernists particularly Foucault, I have come to an understanding that it is important to question certainty in ourselves and others and that it is important to see 'freedom' as 'a constant attempt at self-disengagement and self-invention' (Rajchman quoted in Sawicki, 1991:101). I learnt to draw on my life experiences, to acknowledge them; to examine them; to interpret and reinterpret them in the light of subsequent experience. The story I told then, and indeed am telling now, is only one such partial interpretation; a momentary account which even as I tell it continues to change as a result of the telling.

Having successfully completed my doctorate, I began a new career in academia. In locations such as Trinidad and Tobago and Singapore, I worked with some wonderful and exciting practitioners who were striving to bring education to all in their particular contexts. Inclusion came to mean more to me than special educational needs. Exclusion came in many contexts and guises, and was often embedded in attitudes and practices. Change was challenging for me as for others. As my professional life changed, so too did my personal life. I left a long marriage and began a new relationship, became a mother-in-law, a grandmother. I re-conceptualised my roles as daughter and mother. When I put the last full stop to the hundred thousand words that made up the written thesis, I assumed that it was finished. I little realised that it was in many ways a new beginning but with continuities intertwined and interlaced; old and new complexities and contradictions.

More than 'Just a Mum'

I submitted my thesis for my PhD on March 29 2002. As always, I was pushing it to the line. Only days before I had returned from Singapore where I had been working. I came back to a conference on 27 March, at which I was giving a paper and chairing a session. My thesis was due to be handed in on the 30th. And, to crown it all, I had returned from Singapore with a rumbling toothache which was, I knew, caused by an abscess on a wisdom tooth and, despite my best pleadings to the tooth fairy, was not going to go away by itself.

In the event, I had completed neither the paper nor the dissertion, so spent the two weeks away in a state of panic, alternating between worrying about each of them and consequently improving neither. Never a great long-distance flyer, I spent much of the fourteen hours on the flight back envisaging the awarding of a posthumous doctorate, perceiving this as my only chance of attaining a PhD!

The combination of jet lag, giving a conference paper, chairing a conference session, submitting a doctoral thesis and the pain of an abscess on a wisdom tooth is something I would not wish on anyone. I drove to the conference in a rapidly enveloping mist of pain and jetlag, my main focus being the collection of a horde of pain killing tablets, the stronger the better, and a bottle of whisky with which to down them! I had still not completed my thesis and was two days away from the deadline. The next twenty four hours were spent in the most excruciating blur. I swallowed pain killers rinsed with whisky. Somehow I survived, gave the paper and chaired the session and headed home with only one thought reverberating in my pounding, aching head, get to the dentist! Twenty four hours later, and with one day to go, I had swallowed enough antibiotics to save me from a true rock and roll style exit through drink and drugs. No choice remained now but to get the thesis printed, in triplicate, rush it to the binders, and then dash to the office to submit the thesis by 5.00pm.

My collapse at 5.01pm was complete. I snailed my way home and went to bed. My thesis had taken five and a half years to complete and the journey had not been an easy one.

When I look back on the final days of my thesis, I wonder not only how I did it but why I put myself through such stress, strain, pain and heartache for so many years. Admittedly, the abscess was an unexpected and most unwelcome complication, but why did I, a woman of over fifty, feel driven to give five and a half years of my life to one particular and ultimately personal academic piece of work for public examination by other academics? White (2009) considers the importance of under-standing the various motivations for 'women who are mothers to take up higher education at a stage in their lives when they are also likely to have been involved in a career path and have responsibilities like a mortgage'; how do they remain motivated while there? Her findings suggest that the mothers want to 'improve their employment and finan-cial prospects', 'to improve themselves', and 'to enhance their self-esteem' (White, 2009:80). They want 'to be more than just 'Mum"; to do 'something worthwhile for themselves – to move beyond the boun-daries of their domestic roles' (White, 2009:84-85). I am sure this was true for me too at least in part.

The mad, the bad and the disempowered

Certainly the changes in my life since 1996 when I began my doctoral study have been profound, not only for me but also for my family. They are part of changes which have some continuities with the past; part of wider social and political changes which began long before I was born. But there are also discontinuities for, as Sawicki writes, 'much of history is out of our control ... according to Foucault, our freedom consists in our ability to transform our relationship to tradition and not in being able to control the direction that the future will take' (1991:28). Sawicki continues:

> In part, Foucault's refusal to make any universal political or moral judge-ments is based on the historical evidence that what looks like a change for the better may have undesirable consequences. ...Victories are often over-turned; changes may take on different faces over time. Discourses and institutions are ambiguous and may be utilised for different ends. (1991:27-28)

However, while there may be discontinuities and fractures there can remain underlying resistance to oppression and to dominant dis-courses which can define and boundary. Foucault may have had no utopian vision but Sawicki argues that:

> One need not have an idea of utopia in order to take seriously the injustices in the present. ...In short, genealogy [search for origins] as resistance involves using history to give voice to the marginal and submerged voices which lie, 'a little beneath history', the voices of the mad, the delinquent, the abnormal, the disempowered. It locates many discontinuities and regional struggles against power both in the past and the present. These voices are the sources of resistance, the creative subjects of history. (1991:28)

My doctoral story relates closely to this notion of 'submerged voices' as 'sources of resistance', for the aim of the thesis ultimately was to tell the stories of women whose voices were rarely heard; women who were constructed through powerful discourses around tragedy, denial, rejection and guilt – the mothers and teachers of children often perceived as 'mad', 'delinquent', 'abnormal' and most certainly disempowered. There is a small but growing body of academic work which 'moves away from a simplistic and static conception of the tragic parent of a disabled child' (McLaughlin *et al*, 2008:14), and it is increasingly possible to find published accounts of parents who are extremely positive about their experiences of having a disabled child (eg Murray, 2000, 2003). However, McLaughlin *et al* note that:

> Parents do seem to occupy a no-win situation. They are characterised as either unable to cope or, for those who appear to be coping well, as deluding themselves about the extent of their child's difficulties, sometimes disguising their rejection. (2008:14)

Larson suggests that many parents find themselves in a paradox:

> The management of the internal tension of opposing forces between loving the child as he or she is and wanting to erase the disability, between dealing with the incurability while pursing solutions and between maintaining hopefulness for the child's future while being given negative information and battling their own fears. (Larson, 1998:865)

When I began my study in 1996, my own experiences and an initial search of the literature suggested that the perceptions and feelings of parents, and particularly mothers, were interpreted in pathological ways. McLaughlin *et al* (2008) suggest that this may still be the case. My research indicated that this was true even where the mothers were themselves professionals, 'experts' in a related field.

Mothering is a social practice so is governed by 'certain interests and defined by certain ends' (McLaughlin *et al*, 2008:16) and this particularly seems to be the case for mothers of disabled children who live with a range of disciplinary practices associated with parenting their disabled child. The social construction of such practices is associated with the processes of control through professional power, surveillance and other normative means such as assessment and the 'marketised practices of capitalism' (McLaughlin *et al*, 2008:16).

Yet the mothers in my study all said they rarely if ever talked about their experiences of mothering an impaired child in an exclusionary and disabling society. They felt that they and their children were marginalised and controlled. *Their* discourse was of struggles, fights, battles with professionals, not the language one imagines would illustrate discussions about the wellbeing, care and education of a disabled child. Within these powerful normalising and self regulating discourses Foucault's work seemed to offer ways of interrogating notions of freedom and choice and of challenging professional constructions of mothering. Foucault regarded the powerful discourses underpinning the modern processes of individualisation and normalisation as particularly dangerous; such discourses have constructed the lives of women including mine and the lives of the women in my research.

Past and present struggles and transformations

While there have undoubtedly been social and political changes for women in their roles in families since the Second World War, Miriam David argues that this is as a result of struggle over time and that our

> ... understandings and experiences have increasingly been influenced by those struggling to transform their own lives from the constraints and burdens of past social and economic responsibilities and family and /or sexual obligations. (David, 2003:10)

While my experiences of the 1960s and beyond undoubtedly inform any account of my life, my own PhD story begins in a past before I was born.

I was born in 1949 in the north west of England. My father was a 'company representative' and my mother a primary school teacher. They were both from working class backgrounds but my grandparents had understood the value of education and both had been encouraged and supported by their families in their chosen careers. Two of my grandparents, in particular, have had a significant impact on my own life.

My paternal grandfather Charles was born in the last decade of the nineteenth century in the Isle of Man. At the age of twelve he left for the mainland and settled in Manchester. He married Alice, my grandmother, who stayed at home, it being perceived as the proper thing for an aspiring middle class family to do. They had two sons, Henry (my father) and Alan, both of whom passed their eleven plus examination and attended the local grammar school. When my grandfather retired from work he set out on a fascinating journey of learning and self-discovery which included writing for a crime magazine, learning Spanish and teaching himself Latin! He lived with us for much of my early life and we developed a close and special relationship which was a great source of support to me as I went through the teenage years and on to university. We went to the theatre together to see an eclectic array of plays and concerts. He read widely and conversed with me about my university studies and about historical figures such as Henry Bolingbroke and Johan Van Oldenbarneveldt. He even typed one of my dissertations. One of his few regrets was that he himself had not been to university. He would have loved the Open University and the opportunities it offered but when the first students of the OU began in January 1971 my grandfather was already ill. He died the following year.

My maternal grandmother, Mary Jane, was born in 1892, the youngest of six children from a Welsh speaking mining family. In her early teens my grandmother left the valleys and headed for the industrial north west of England to take her chances in the cotton mills of Lancashire. In 1919, she married James and there followed two children, Jack and my mother Marie (born 1927). My grandmother firmly believed in the education of women as a way out of the hard and often dangerous life in the cotton mills. When my mother gained a scholarship to the local grammar school (the one my father and uncle had attended), my grandmother was determined to support her and even saved to buy her a piano, which entailed huge family sacrifice. My mother studied music at college and became a primary school teacher, following one of the traditional ways to rise out of poverty and the working classes for women at that time. When my grandmother died in 1966 at the age of

74, I was doing my O-level GCEs at the same grammar school that my mother, father and uncle had attended.

As I moved through the years of compulsory schooling, I never questioned the value of education or school. I accepted it, and in many ways, enjoyed it, as an only child loving the companionship of school, but also respecting and valuing, if not always understanding, the clear belief of my parents that it had something to offer me for the future. Firm friendships were formed during these school years which remain strong today. Without realising it we all supported each other. We were described by our teachers as 'lively' and were in many ways challenging to our parents and teachers but we were generally described as 'good girls' who valued the acquisition of qualifications and who wanted to go onto to higher education. However, I think sometimes we made the journey a little more exciting than perhaps our parents and teachers would have wished and often managed a show of resistance!

But I don't think we ever really questioned what lay beyond formal education. In retrospect, I realise that within these expectations was the firmly held belief that we would also marry and raise families; in other words become good wives and mothers. My father believed that teaching was a good job for a woman as it enabled her to have a family life, a career (job?), make a contribution to the family income and have some independence. In short, I was to be and do what my mother had done so successfully before me. My father had been born in the 1920s and brought up in the inter war era, when one of the beliefs of many lower middle class men had been that it was an indicator of family improvement if the woman remained at home as a 'good' wife and mother. My mother's job as a primary school teacher fell into a post war perspective that it was OK for her to be in the respectable, caring professions – like nursing, secretarial work or teaching – as a primary school teacher. But she was still expected to take on complete responsibility for the home and the people in it.

My own developing awareness of the world beyond my small corner began in January 1961 with the inauguration of John F. Kennedy as president of the USA and of course his assassination on November 22 1963. Closer to home, the Profumo Affair (1963), and the apparent glamour and notoriety of Christine Keeler and Mandy Rice Davies mesmerised us as teenagers with our gradually awakening sense of the 'hush hush', and our developing awareness of our own sexualities. The Moors murders perhaps affected us more profoundly (1963-1965), for we lived near to Saddleworth Moor. These murders were referred to in some media reports at the time as the end of the 'age of innocence' when parents could let their children play out of sight. Such events, especially those so near to home, sliced into the relatively secluded world of our single sex girls' grammar school and inevitably informed our experiences of 'growing up' .

Good vibrations: the discourses we live by – good girls, good wives, good mothers'

On the whole my friends and I focused on our work, our growing interest in boys and sex and all things related to Dusty Springfield, Cathy Mcgowan, and Marianne Faithful. We worshipped the Beatles, the Rolling Stones, and the Beach Boys. We went away on holiday on our own, ten of us in a flat in Bournemouth and had the time of our lives. As the decade wore on we upped our resistance to parental norms and our skirts to the miniest of minis. Our boyfriends were Mods with scooters and parkers. I don't think we had any notion of marrying these boys, friends of our friend's twin brother, but enjoyed their companionship and the relative safety of sexual exploration with them. It was generally accepted that the boys were expected to 'try', and we good girls were expected to say 'no'. Despite the decade being proclaimed one of free love and the pill, the latter was not readily available for grammar school girls of sixteen or seventeen at that time, and the risk of pregnancy before marriage was not one we wanted to take.

I dutifully and not unwillingly went successfully through the examination system and on to University in the autumn of 1968 on my nineteenth birthday, to study contemporary history and English. It was the year of student rebellions across the UK and Europe, and I was excited at the thought of being a part of something moving, stirring, struggling. While at university, I don't recall being taught history by any women and certainly all the professors in the history department were men. The ratio of male students to female across the whole university was something like 4:1. We had an inspiring and amazing woman teacher for English at A-level and I had expected the same degree of intensity and passion at university but somehow it did not materialise. It was to be some time before the sense of liberation and excitement through formal learning was to return.

I declared myself a feminist and argued about equal pay for woman, sex discrimination and sexual harassment. As I searched for a job I was made very aware of gender pay differentials and the prejudice against young women of child-bearing age, despite a number of social welfare policies relating to women's welfare (eg the 1967 Abortion Act, the Equal Pay Act 1970, the Sex Discrimination Act 1975). There was no acknowledgement that more women were returning to work very soon after having their children or leaving having children till they had established careers (David, 2003:62). We were expected to be mothers and penalised for it. Yet looking back, my friends and I fulfilled our families' expectations admirably. To quote the wonderful words of Mandy Rice Davies, we made our own 'slow descent into respectability'!

I opted for a Post Graduate Certificate of Education and by September 1972 I was teaching in a purpose built comprehensive school in Berkshire. By 1979 I was married and a full time mother of two. I had ticked most of the normative boxes! I don't know if at this time I consciously felt the power of dominant discourses and societal norms driving me in this direction. It was just what many women in my situation did: we became housewives and mothers, nurturing and caring and of course, self-sacrificing, supporting the breadwinners in their careers. I loved being at home with my two small children, but I was made aware that for some this did not constitute work as it was unpaid and in the home; no credit would be given for it as it was seen as a labour of love. Anyone who has remained at home with small children will relate to Pillay's experience that, while the sheer joy of loving your own children is beyond compare, the 'unending responsibility' involved in the daily care of babies and children can be all consuming (Pillay, 2007:4). The importance of motherhood seemed to be at one and the same time revered as self sacrificing but dismissed as natural; it was what women as mothers did.

Motherhood, education, difference and disability

In 1979 Margaret Thatcher became the first woman Prime Minister and, as David notes, 'These political events framed our thinking and teaching and enabled us to develop both new substantive agendas about women's involvement in public life and new pedagogies around personal experience' (2003:62). Yet as I settled down to life with two small children, these changes did not seem to impact on my daily life.

I had grown up on a diet of *Janet and John* reading books in the 1950s which reflected the gendered values of the time; Janet helped mother in the kitchen while John was in the garage or garden with father. I was also a child of the welfare state, growing up with free health care, milk and orange juice. Wilson (1977) argues that the welfare state reinforced these family discourses:

> Only feminism has made it possible for us to see how the state defines femininity and that this definition is not marginal but is central to the purposes of welfarism. Woman is above all Mother, and with this vocation go all the virtues of femininity; submission, nurturance passivity. The 'feminine' client of the social services waits patiently at clinics, social security offices, and housing departments, to be administered to sometimes by the paternal authority figure, doctor or civil servant, sometimes by the nurturant yet firm model of femininity provided by nurse or social worker; in either case she goes away to do as she has been told – to take the pills, to love the baby. (Wilson, 1977:7-8)

I can certainly identify with this. I (Cole, 2004), along with others (eg Pillay, 2007; Sikes, 1997), have argued that being a mother changes your life. In my own case, the changes were profound. I have already described what happened to my son at the age of thirteen months. This meant that my life, just as Wilson outlines above, involved endless trips to assessment clinics, physiotherapy units, hospitals, health clinics etc. I waited for home visits, hospital appointments, clinicians, health visitors, therapists. As I wrote in my thesis:

> Peace was the first thing to go; the peace that comes on a rainy afternoon when a baby is sleeping and a small child is engrossed, playing contentedly. ... A whole army of professionals now descended on us: speech therapists, social workers, and medical professionals. If the house was chaotic, it somehow now mattered whereas it hadn't before. I felt judged on my performance as a mother. It seemed there were queues of people waiting to assess Graham, and by implication, me! How much had we done this week? What progress had we made? ...There seemed to be little doubt in the minds of the professionals that a 'good' mother of a disabled child would be ready at all times for the professionals, who were coming to 'help'. (Cole, 2002:22)

Graham attended the same local primary school as his sister. For the first term he went into the class of a truly inclusive teacher, who tried hard to include him in everything the class did but, unfortunately, with the new January intake of children he had to change classes and moved into the class of a teacher with very different views who, along with the headteacher, felt that Graham should attend a special school. They made their views known through some peevish and unpleasant behaviour against this small child who was doing his best to be a part of the school. The situation was resolved when we moved because of my husband's work. Graham now went to the village school with his sister, where he was accepted as one of the village children. This was in 1984 and the policy context was beginning to change around us. We were soon to be further embroiled in these changes.

The changing policy context: a fish out of water

The 1981 Education Act (DES, 1981) was now coming into effect, bringing in many of the recommendations of the Warnock Report on special educational needs (DES, 1978). One of the main changes was the introduction of the Statement of Special Educational Need, the aim of which was to identify needs and 'guarantee' local authority funding for any child diagnosed as 'having' special educational needs and 'wherever possible' children would be educated along with their peers in mainstream settings. There remain serious criticisms, contradictions and tensions around the intentions, findings and implementation of the Warnock Report and the 1981 Education Act which followed. Baroness Warnock herself has criticised statementing, although for different reasons from some of her critics. Whatever the intentions, a statement was meant to provide funding for individual children and to accompany them wherever they went. Local authorities, however, were taking up to a year to complete the process and were becoming increasingly reluctant – and unable – to provide funds.

The changes in special education were taking place within other, far reaching changes in general education policy. The 1988 Education Reform Act (DES, 1988) began the relentless move towards developing a quasi market in education in which it was claimed that parental choice, informed by a range of performance indicators, would drive up standards. A new inspection regime, in the form of Ofsted, was set up, which had a remit to name and shame 'failing' schools. Children who were perceived as different and as not contributing to a higher place in the league tables were now often unwelcome. A statement of special educational need, if indeed one were obtained, could be seen by mainstream schools as a warning sign. As the 1980s moved to a close amidst battles between local authorities, trade unions and the government, I was becoming more aware of how the changes in the educational context were impacting on both my professional and personal life. I was as yet unaware of how sharply they would bring me into the feminist world of the 'personal as political'.

The personal and the political

In the mid 1980s I went back to teaching in a mainstream 11-18 comprehensive school in Shropshire, working with students with statements of special educational needs. I was working across the school with pupils who were often on the edge of exclusion for a variety of reasons. As league tables kicked in, the school was perceived as struggling and the Ofsted report was not good.

This was the secondary school Graham would come to but for many reasons we felt that this might not be the best place for him. I did some research about schools, dug my heels in with the Local Education Authority (LEA), and after twelve months struggle it was agreed that Graham would attend a wonderful special school in the area. Graham and I have often reflected together on this decision, which was mine and his father's rather than his, although he remains sure that the school was the best choice for him at the time. However, while it offered Graham many opportunities he would certainly never have had at the comprehensive school, it did isolate him from local friends and as time went by he felt increasingly marginalised by some of the processes which labelled him as 'different'.

This was around the early 1990s and it began a period of considerable concern and doubt for me as to what was happening in education and in my own particular context. For parents who wanted a mainstream education for their child who was perceived as different, a fight lay ahead. This was equally true for children whose parents sought funding or a place at a special school. It seemed to be a lose-lose situation for them. While education policies loudly proclaimed the power of 'parental choice', it appeared as if such power was vested in very few. Certainly for the parents of impaired children or those diagnosed as having 'special educational needs' there seemed to be little real parent power. Despite the rhetoric and number of policies supporting inclusion (eg DfEE, 1994, 1997a, 1997b, 1997c, 1998a; DfES, 2001, 2002, 2004), it was the standards' agenda which provided the dominant context. For those of us working with children perceived as challenging, especially in some secondary schools, the tensions and contradictions of these two policy initiatives created an extremely difficult context in which to work. In 1994, I worked with others to meet the requirements of the Code of Practice for Special Educational Needs as we prepared for an Ofsted inspection. By 1995, I felt I was working in a very difficult and tense environment; I was uncomfortable professionally and personally and so I left the school.

It is not always an easy road to travel being a teacher and a mother, let alone the mother of a child perceived as different. Working in a secondary school, I was well aware of the pressure on teachers' children. A number of teachers had children in the school and on the whole these children were considered good and usually successful in examinations. I was equally aware of how difficult it was for some other children to escape from their label of difference – and how once labelled, they were perceived to *be* so. Staff would return to the staffroom after a difficult lesson and some would loudly lay the blame on one or two children who were known by all the staff, whether or not they taught them. Some of the names these children were called were far from flattering, pathologising and marginalising the child. I did not want this to be Graham.

As it was I frequently found myself, like many other mothers of disabled children, in a battle with the local authority or with medical and quasi medical professionals, who seemed to completely discount my role, experience and voice as a mother. It struck me as strange that when I described meetings with medical 'experts' and some educational professionals the language was reminiscent of war, and words such as 'fight', 'struggle' 'battle' etc. were common. I know I am not alone in this experience (Cole, 2004).

Yet I have also had the privilege of working with and knowing some inspiring teachers; teachers who valued and supported difference. Some of the most supportive teachers were in the special school Graham attended. What I did not fully appreciate until later is how the education system itself excludes so many children; how it is designed to ensure that many children will not be successful at school and their life chances will consequently be limited; how the curriculum excludes many children and how particular pedagogies and organisational cultures reinforce this. I naively thought that comprehensive education had something to offer to support the learning of every child. So when I left school teaching in 1995, I was becoming increasingly disillusioned with what I was trying to do as a teacher within the changing education policy context.

I decided to return to formal learning myself and embarked on an MA in Educational Management. I found myself struggling to read, write and think in a way I had not had to do for almost twenty five years. My daughter was doing her A-levels, and needing considerable support and encouragement. Graham was wondering what he would do on reaching school leaving age and experiencing considerable frustration that his options seemed limited. I suffered the feelings of stress and guilt felt by women 'organising their own children before and after school, spending more time away from the home, and relying on the support of other people to care for their children' (White, 2009:90).

I managed to do some work in the day but much of it was done after 10.30pm when the house began to quieten down. I often worked until 3.am or later and was up again before 6.30am to get two reluctant teenagers to school, feed and muck out and sometimes exercise two horses, feed dogs and cats and decide what to feed everyone else on their return. The evenings could be fraught. This was a time when Graham was experiencing ever stronger epileptic fits and increased frustration which often manifested itself in quite violent arguments with other members of the family. As my husband was working away from home, there was little choice for me but to deal with *all* things domestic as well as the MA. There is now a body of literature which substantiates the claim that women still take on the primary role of caring within the family (David, 1993; 2000; Reay, 2005), regardless of their outside roles and can suffer stress and guilt as a consequence. There is also research to suggest that fathers who return to HE do not have the same sense of guilt as mothers (Thompson, 2000).

I certainly never considered doing a doctorate and when the opportunity presented itself, it was entirely serendipitous; a matter of momentary chance and challenge which, after only one evening of deep and solitary contemplation, I decided to meet head on. It seemed too ridiculous for words. Me, doing a PhD? What was I thinking of! I was a mother, a disillusioned school teacher, an unhappy wife. I was not a Doctor of Philosophy! But the thought remained; me doing a PhD? Goodness me!

I did not realise it at the time just how pivotal that evening of decision making was for me. I was making a decision which was to take me way outside my comfort zone and I don't think I have ever returned to it since! My friends thought I was going through a mid life crisis. I suppose was! I was very unhappy in my marriage and felt this might offer one way to open up my life, to open up new opportunities. It certainly did. It literally changed my life, personally and professionally, and although I did not realise it at the time, was to introduce me to a new partner, new friends, new career and new ways of thinking, feminist thinking around the 'personal as political'.

The personal as political

And so I have returned to almost where I began this chapter. In March 2002 I completed my PhD, to the delight of my family and friends. But I cannot end the chapter here, for if I do the real essence of it would be missing. For ultimately it was not about five and a half years of academic work, or achieving a PhD. I have been writing about changes, the political and social changes which underpin the story told here and which have, in both obvious and more subtle ways, impacted on my life. What happened to me in that time was that my personal and professional lives collided or, perhaps more accurately, synergised. Slowly my study became about my life and my life experiences informed the study. When I began my PhD I set out to research issues related to the funding and management of special educational needs. When I handed in my thesis it told stories of mothers who were teachers of children perceived as different; it told my story as well. I was learning to '*use [my] life experiences in [my] intellectual work*' as Mills had recommended (1970: 216).

I changed not only what I was doing but the way I wanted to do it. My study used a narrative research approach, drawing on lived experience as a way of challenging powerful discourses which can boundary and define. After a rather shaky and unfocused beginning, my new supervisor gave me Dorothy Smith's (1987) seminal book to read, along with Ann Oakley's *The Sociology of Housework* (1974), and I began reading. I gave her Pat Sikes's *Parents who Teach* (1997) and we began to understand where I wanted to go with my research.

During the five and half years of doctoral study, my life changed in ways I could not have envisaged. I left my marriage of twenty five years and moved out of the marital home and into a room in student accommodation, followed by a house sit, and then into rented accommodation. At the age of fifty these did not feel like easy changes. I was at the same time frightened and excited by them. I met my partner, and my PhD companion, Molly – a feisty west highland white terrier. I got my first full time academic job – which I loved – at the University of Sheffield and was greatly privileged to work in Singapore, the Caribbean and the UK with amazing educational professionals and academic colleagues from and through whom I continue to grow.

I am currently a Senior Lecturer in Inclusive Education at the Institute of Education, University of London, teaching on the MA in Inclusive Education and researching into different aspects of inclusion and exclusion. I am also the Faculty Director of Post Graduate Research for the Faculty of Policy and Society, which currently has around 350 doctoral students studying for both the Doctorate in Education (EdD) and PhDs. Many of these students are women, both home students and international students, part-time and full-time, and of all ages. Many of them are engaged in feminist study and will explore their own professional and personal experiences as the basis for their academic work, drawing on different theories for understanding and support. For many of them it will be a challenging time, creating unexpected shifts, changes and uncertainties, and inevitably some of these will be difficult to negotiate. For some their lived experiences will ultimately inform their studies and be researched and reflected upon through different methodological approaches and theoretical perspectives.

Foucault, narrative, the PhD and me: the right to be uncertain

In my own academic work I try to retain the complexity of lived experience by struggling to use narrative approaches to research because I believe they can offer significant insights into how we understand ourselves and how we make meaning in our lives. As my career in higher education has progressed and through my work with practitioners and other academics, I have come to understand the terms 'inclusion' and 'exclusion' very differently. I am increasingly aware of the power of discourse to construct and marginalise unless critiqued and resisted, an awareness which demands important but often uncomfortable personal challenges. I believe narrative offers possibilities for recognising resistance and alternative discourses.

I wrote earlier about some of the discourses which I felt had constrained and constructed my own life; normative discourses which sought to produce 'good girls', 'good wives' and 'good mothers'. I am now very conscious that there are powerful discourses which construct what it is to be a 'good academic'; a 'good female academic'; and a 'good academic mother' (see Pillay, 2007). Powerful and normative discourses abound in higher education, constructing and constraining the academic community and the women who seek to belong to it, many of whom seek to use their own lived experiences as the basis of their work. There are still considerable risks in opening up our own life experiences as the subject for academic study, and in using narrative in educational research. There is always the risk of accusations of solipsism and self indulgence.

But a serious risk is emerging, as noted by Lyons (2007:600). She argues that, while in the US there has been a growth of narrative approaches over the last thirty years, there is at the same time a 'narrowing' of what is perceived as 'valid educational research'. Lyons maintains that in the US scientifically based research (SBR) involving research based on experimental designs and randomised trials is increasingly becoming known as the gold standard. Such research is attracting the funding and, given the international nature of much educational and social research, is having an impact on research in other countries too including the UK (Lyons, 2007:602). Bringing in funding to the HE institution is increasingly an important part of the work of an academic. Given the recent world financial situation, what will count as 'proper' educational research in the UK and how will this constrain and construct what it means in the second decade of the 21st century to be a successful academic? How might this impact on feminist research approaches? How will it constrain what is counted as social science research?

Narrative accounts told within historical, political and sociological contexts can illuminate hidden oppression, exclusion and powerful dominant discourses which 'other' and marginalise. They can offer spaces for resistance and counter narratives, narratives of difference as diversity rather than deviance, narratives which highlight the gaps, the intersectionalities of race, gender, disability, class, sexuality, age, religion etc; and the shifting of positionalities and sites of power. Writing in this way is not easy or comfortable. It can involve the researcher as researched and throws into stark relief a range of ethical issues: issues of confidentiality, anonymity, truth, memory recall, bias, objectivity, selectivity of data, evaluation, and so on. But it can challenge hidden assumptions and the certainties on which many so-called common sense notions are held.

In this chapter I have briefly explored some of the discourses and societal constructions in relation to my own life and experiences; experiences of normativity, difference, disability and normalisation, inclusion and exclusion and motherhood, and powerful professional and expert claims to knowledge. When I began my doctoral research I did not question terms such as 'special educational needs' and my view then was that the government did not fund it properly, but merely paid lip service to it. As a mother, I was caught in Larson's paradox, noted earlier, swinging from one position to the other. I felt my 'mother's voice' was unheard and my professional voice politically irrelevant. However, as my ideas began to develop through my research, I found the experience liberating. I was a practitioner and in the context of the PhD research I had to engage with theoretical ideas to underpin my experiences. I began to find theoretical support and insights in the work of Foucault, who does 'not tell us what to do, but rather how some of our ways of thinking and doing are historically linked to particular forms of power and social control' (Sawicki, 1991:47). Sawicki writes:

> As feminists I believe that we have good reason to appeal to Foucault's negative freedom, that is the freedom to disengage from our political identities,

our presumptions about gender differences, and the categories and practices that define feminism. We must cultivate this freedom because feminism
has developed in the context of oppression. Women are produced by patriar-
chal power at the same time they resist it. (Sawicki, 1991:102)

Doctoral research has been both liberating and constraining. I often feel way outside my comfort zone in academia as a relative newcomer struggling to explore the complexities which abound in issues related to inclusion and exclusion. But it has given me a new and invigorating life when many people of my age may be thinking about retirement, and here am I, trying to push at boundaries rather than the lawn mower – or daisies – while still trying to grapple with Foucault! It is scary stuff but I am enjoying the right to be uncertain.

4

Researching Life Itself: human centred passionate appreciation

Gloria Gordon

Introduction: knowledge and change

> Know that many personal troubles cannot be solved merely as troubles, but must be understood in terms of public issues and in terms of the problems of history-making. Know that the human meaning of public issues must be revealed by relating them to personal troubles and to the problems of the individual life. Know that the problems of social science, when adequately formulated, must include both troubles and issues, both biography and history, and the range of their intricate relations. (C Wright Mills, 1959:226)

My PhD studies (Bravette, 1997) followed on directly from the completion of my MBA research project (Bravette, 1993), in which I explored the experience of being black in organisational/institutional life, with the goal of achieving transformational outcomes. I doubt I would have a PhD today had I not adopted the practitioner/researcher approach, with the sole aim of exploring the lived contradictions of being 'black' in British society. At the time I had little understanding of the link between personal troubles and public issues, as noted by C Wright Mills. Instead I saw myself as the problem and continually thought of ways of ending my life, little realising that what I was experiencing was death to a way of being. Having a witnessing nature and being situated on the periphery of British society in an insider/outsider position meant I was acutely aware of the contradictions between what is espoused publicly and what actually happens where race is concerned as a social issue. I was tired of being 'black' and certainly did not want my children – I am the mother of three sons – to live through the black experience as I was then living it.

Autobiographical research linked to institutional biography was to be the challenging path I took to such understanding. There was, I felt, a missing piece in the jigsaw of the human experience where the experience of descendants of enslaved Africans (DoEAs), otherwise referred to as black Caribbean or black British, are concerned. I needed to get to the bottom of it. Black in the context of this chapter refers specifically to DoEAs, the group that identifies as members of the 'black community' and 'black culture'. This is as opposed to those who belong to ethnic minority groups or cultures but identify as 'black' to signify exploitative and oppressive life experiences and relations.

My Master's and PhD research were, therefore, at their core about developing competence in understanding my life as a member of the 'black community' – different, excluded and unequal. Engagement, as opposed to avoidance with the black British Caribbean experience ultimately led me to a realisation of the human experience and the dysfunctionality of the black experience. At the time I personally needed to understand why my life was 'sensitive' and a taboo subject (Frankenberg, 1993; Thomas, 1989) in the university context where I worked, as well as in the wider social context. Also, what was behind the silence that surrounds race as an issue? I was seeking self-knowledge and awareness of what it means to be a whole human being but, unaware of this at the time, I started with the 'black' label that was negatively attributed to me.

Although my choice to research my racialised identity was not a popular one, I was at the time experiencing a strong generative desire (Kotre, 1983) to create an improved legacy for future generations. Given the wasteland I understood my life to be I had no qualms in using it as a means of drawing lessons for future generations. Instinctively, I understood that if I continued to avoid 'race' as an issue I would be failing an important life challenge and, more importantly, I would be leaving in place barriers for my own children and students to face in the future. This suggests that my doctoral study was at this time less about developing an academic career within Higher Education and more about developing knowledge to transform lives, starting with my own. I remember Sivanandan's (1974:110) view of knowledge inspiring me at the time:

> ... knowledge is not a goal in itself, but a path to wisdom; it bestows not privilege so much as duty, not power so much as responsibility. It brings with it a desire to learn even as one teaches, to teach even as one learns. It is used not to compete with one's fellow beings for some unending standard of life, but to achieve for them, as for oneself, a higher quality of life.

Making the choice to use my life-world, personal and professional, as the research terrain allowed me to contain the risks – triggering racialised emotions, misuse of power, backlash, etc – involved in researching the black experience because of any perceived threats to the racial *status quo*. The extent of the existential crisis in which I existed at the time meant I ignored warnings of possible careercide. I was, I felt, already at the bottom of the pile and did not see there was any lower to fall.

Background (1959-1989)
I arrived in England from Jamaica in 1959 at the age of five with my older sister, Grace, to join our parents and our new sibling, Doreen. My father had been recruited by companies seeking labour from the Caribbean in 1954 and so had left Jamaica before my birth. The country was hostile to the black presence in 1959 and it was in this context that we we find ourselves placed in a local infant school in Brixton, London. My earliest memories of school are of an environment in which I did not fit. This is although there were lots of other black children there. Although this theme of not fitting was to become a life theme for me, at that time I did not fit because the white teachers largely saw us black children as strangers and often spoke about us as if we were not present and could not hear. I picked up the clear message of being unwanted and undesirable.

This experience led me to find ways of being accepted. The strategy I adopted, not associating with other black children in school, was effective but was not in any way mediated in the home or school. In fact it was rewarded in the school context. This mode of being became problematic over the years, as the mask of the 'good black girl' I developed began to crack even as I equally resented that this mask was necessary at all. A defining experience of my location in the school context is seen in the following experience: whilst queuing up for a lunch, a group of black girls decided to storm the queue and push in front of us. My best friend responded to this saying: 'look at those ignorant black bastards!' Seconds later she turned to me and said: 'not you Gloria, you are different'. I was, however, keenly aware of being black, despite my strategy of not associating with other black children at school.

Over time it became apparent to me that I had to maintain this way of being to be acceptable to white teachers and friends; it was not a choice that could be changed without consequences. A series of critical incidents made it evident that I was not to acknowledge a different perspective on the social context if I did not want to risk rejection, even though I saw and experienced the world differently. As a consequence, I became silent even as I was being silenced. This experience took place in a national and worldwide context where black people were struggling for their rights, not least Martin Luther King and Malcolm X, both of whom were to meet violent deaths.

My own experience closer to home had taught me that I had little in the way of rights and needed to appease the white majority if I did not want to be sent back from whence I came. As this underlying experience of scant or non-expression continued into my late thirties, I found myself in an existential crisis of meaning while employed in higher education. I used the requirement placed on staff to gain higher qualifications in the late 1980s to pursue postgraduate studies to initially gain parity with my white peers and only because this strategy continued to fail did I finally make the decision to engage with the issues and experience.

PhD studies: the action turn

I found Reason's (2001) idea that we need to take an 'action turn' toward studying ourselves in action in relation to others a challenging necessity. Not fully understanding what this meant resulted in my naively entering a path where angels might well fear to tread. My masters' research had identified silence, understandable as the slow slipping into a kind of invisible isolation, a significant issue for me. To work with this experience I selected first person action research, one of three transformational strategies offered by Reason (2001), as the most

66

appropriate means of working with myself as well as managing the problem of racialised emotions (Martinas, 1992). First person action research/inquiry involves first person, primarily subjective research of individuals inquiring in the midst of everyday life and practice. Use of the action turn revealed me as deeply implicated in the circumstances of the life outcomes I so detested. The process resulted in a meeting with an unexpected other: my self. It also revealed that I had legitimate reasons for blocking insights as to the unconscious choices I was making, as seen in the bicultural competence matrix discussed later.

In effect the use of action research led me to become a social anthropologist and forensic scientist, interrogating my own life world in the context of the wider systems of which I am a part. I recall being shocked into speechlessness and pain as I began to understand how the black and white identities, as we know them today, created in slavery, were dynamically constructed and reconstructed within the invisible institution of culture and of how I had been socialised to be unconsciously complicit in the process. I had accepted Reason's (2001) challenge for engagement in a mode of research that moves us

> ... toward a kind of research/practice open in principle to anyone willing to commit to integrating inquiry and practice in everyday personal and professional settings. In fact, we all inevitably integrate inquiry and practice *implicitly* in our everyday conduct. Nevertheless, the call to integrate inquiry and practice both explicitly and implicitly in our everyday conduct represents a demand that few persons in history have attempted to accept. (p5)

The challenges of the commitment to integrate inquiry and practice *explicitly* in my everyday conduct is a series of books still to be written, as I began to understand the massive gap between choice, black culture and what it means to be a whole, fully alive, experiencing, choiceful human being. No dimension of my life-world was left untouched as I came into self knowledge. For the first time in my life I was to appreciate the process via which slavery results in social death (Patterson, 1982) across generations and why the legacies of slavery are so far-reaching in terms of their impact still today (Bales, 1999). The challenges of the PhD caused me to speed up the process, completing in three years, so that I could move beyond it. Little did I realise this would be an impossibility.

Reason (2001:12) used my PhD as an exemplar of first person action research in his own analysis of the action turn acknowledging that:

> Gloria Bravette's PhD thesis (1997) provides an account of one woman's personal inquiry into her 'life-world' enabling her to engage in a self-conscious process of transformation from total identification with Anglo norms to a dialectical 'bicultural competence.' In the course of her research, Bravette engages with a whole range of ways of knowing – experiential, pre-sentational, propositional, and practical. Experientially, she gradually confronts her introjection of the white racist perspective which encourages her to deny her 'blackness' in an attempt to be 'one of us,' while at the same time experiencing herself as inferior:
>
>> (I) did not have a sound identity or sense of self, the result of not being culturally grounded... This is despite the fact that I had been successfully recruited into white UK culture through educational socialisation since the age of five. Living the contradictions of the culture as espoused, as a black person, had prevented that successful recruitment, however. What I have painfully come to realise is that culture is in fact group/race and history specific and that as an African (the correct label for me) I had been 'culturally misoriented'... in that I had been educated into a western culture that was not my own .... (Bravette, 1997:46)

It is interesting for me to read Reason's analysis of my work four years after gaining my doctorate and to consider my current position as a consequence of where persistent use of the action turn has brought me. In 1997 I saw no alternative to the prison of 'blackness'. By 2001, when Reason's article was published, I had moved on towards an achieved identity (Marcia, 1966) and referred to myself as *African Caribbean British* as I began to gain insights into the significance of the identity formation process. In 2009, I refer to myself as *British African Caribbean* as a consequence of coming into the realisation of the significant impact British culture has had on my life experience as well as who I am. Today I recognise and acknowledge my ancestral lineage and have accepted responsibility for integrating the three disparate, even oppositional, cultures that make up my unique cultural heritage. One of the many gifts that I now realise has always been present in the life challenges that is presented to DoEAs, like myself, is that captured in the words of C L R James (cited by Procter, 2000:63):

The black man or woman who is born here and grows up here has something special to contribute to western civilisations. He or she will participate
in it, see it from birth, but will never be quite completely in it. What such
persons have to say, therefore, will give a new vision, a deeper and stronger
insight into both western civilisation and the black people in it.

Silent and silenced as a black member of society, without community
and a culture of origin, I was unable to realise this and other gifts,
having nowhere to bring them and no one to receive them (Some,
2008). It is this silenced experience that allows slavery, of which African
slavery was the first phase (Unesco, 2000) to be a growing industry in
the global economy (Bales, 1999).

From black socialisation to authentic human development

As an educator I now realise I was the recipient of 'black socialisation',
the process whereby significant segments of the human family are
socialised into powerlessness (Lukes, 1974). Enslaved Africans and their
descendants were specifically targeted for this treatment through
slavery and colonisation. As I have said, my education had been filled
with fear and anxiety as I sought to appease white teachers so as to ensure I did not end up in the bottom streams or even become labelled as
an educationally subnormal (ESN) child in the 1960s. If Palmer (1997) is
correct in his reminder that teaching is no other than the elemental
bond that exists between the elder of the tribe and their young then I
have lost out. I have never been formally taught by an elder of my own
tribe. For black children this bond has been broken and remains broken
in plural societies like Britain where the reciprocal role relating outcomes between blacks and whites, which work to perpetuate psychological slavery, continue largely unquestioned. What the slavery
relationship elicits for 'blacks' is a sense of powerlessness, victimhood
and lack of self-efficacy. I came to recognise the socialisation process as
one in which the mind and consciousness is shaped. This pointed to
differential black and white socialisation being not only historical but
very much contemporary also.

In my pre-doctoral research life I had been locked into a 'foreclosed'
(Marcia, 1966) black identity the result of living within the constraints of
an unconscious black culture, described by McWhorter (2001) as an
externally imposed cultural disorder that has taken on a life of its own.

These black and white identities are institutionalised as seen in the ethnic classification used by the Office for National Statistics (ONS, 2003). Rarely acknowledged is the fact that black culture is an offspring of the institution of slavery and the invisible institution of the culture which spawned slavery in the first place and which still operates to keep it in place. My education to this point had been limited to the 'black socialisation', administered by members of both black communities and white, and critical to the maintenance of a dysfunctional black culture (Gordon, 2006).

The five dimensional human being model I developed (Gordon, 2007), the result of scrutinising the knowledge of the time before African slavery, revealed the problem starkly in terms of the human cost of slavery. The crisis of meaning I had been undergoing was, it seems, a consequence of outgrowing the limitations of the externally imposed cultural disorder of black culture, including silence, which was constraining my growth. Black culture was crystallised as a fixed structural component of British culture as opposed to a culture external to British culture as it is problematised to be. In fact Tisdell's (2000) conceptualisation of the term 'politics of positionality' describes the relationship that exists between blacks and whites well. The outcome: as a black child in the 1960s I was unconsciously assimilated into black British culture, a hidden subculture of British culture, consisting of a familiar reciprocal role relating a way of being which had operated since the 16th century. It is a way of being that both parties know well and continue to refine both consciously and unconsciously.

Coming into this conscious awareness my challenge was that of self-reconstruction, beginning with my transformation perspective in terms of what it means to be human. It seems that the human task involves the integration of the physical, mental, emotional and spiritual achieved through the fifth dimension, culture, as illustrated in figure 1.

I found that as a DoEA, the white ethnic majority had ownership of the fifth dimension, culture, ensuring they also had ownership in my interior world. The outcomes of this are shown in figure 2.

McWhorter's conceptualisation of black culture, an externally imposed cultural disorder which has taken on a life of its own, made perfect sense. It went a long way towards explaining the psychic disorientation,

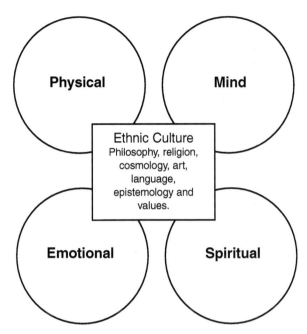

Figure 1 – The five dimensional human being

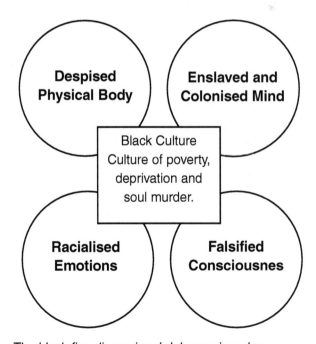

Figure 2 – The black five dimensional dehumaniser doer

confusion and despair I write about in my own book (Gordon, 2007). Pinderhughes (1979) describes it as a culture of victimhood and Painter (1995), building on Schengold's (1989) work, as 'soul murder'. Banton's (1997) differentiation between groups that exist as a 'social category' as opposed to a functioning minority ethnic group explains well the positioning of the black community in British society, as shown in figure 3 below.

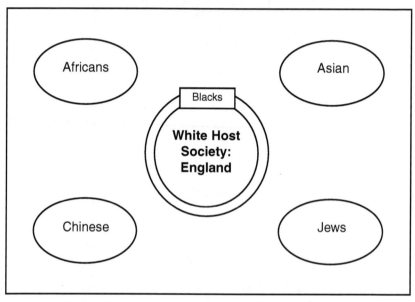

Figure 3 – How Britain manages its diversity

The action research/inquiry approach I adopted was, therefore, crucial to my research goals, demanding as it did the integration of theory with practice as I worked with this new knowledge to bring about the desired interior perspective transformation that would change external outcomes for me. My PhD process thus facilitated the ripping of the 'racial veil' of black/white cultures that had been instrumental in blurring my vision. Starkly revealed were the social forces involved, as well as how I had unconsciously been co-opted into black British culture at the periphery of the white host society and culture. Choice was to become a significant theme as I experienced for the first time the demand for real choice: whether to carry on in a dysfunctional life diminishing relationship or to step up to a new way of being.

A new way of being meant making the decision to become a conscious creator of culture in my own right and brought about a conscious and deliberate transition from a dysfunctional black *racial* identity to a British African Caribbean *ethnic* identity, and thus culture, of my own choosing. I moved towards becoming a generative actor, acting to bring about change by responding contrary to the normative values of the society. This changed mode of being required much courage as I consciously began to act with agency in a way I had never done before. I had effectively moved to the place of what I term 'authentic human development'. I was only now, in my 40s, learning how to be a conscious creator of culture in my own right – the human task that enslaved Africans and their dependants have been deprived of as a consequence of slavery/colonisation.

Conscious autodidactic education

Engaging in active reconstructive work led to the emergence of a new self, a rebirth. The bicultural competence matrix I developed (figure 4 below) shows how I had been born – as are all children – onto the top left quadrant of *unconscious bicultural incompetence*. On this quadrant we are dependent on significant others (parents and teachers) to nurture us into consciousness and movement across the matrix, to *conscious bicultural incompetence* whereby we learn the importance of taking responsibility for our own learning as a result of the curiosity that has hopefully been engendered. Given, however, the imperfections of our world, I, like many people, moved from the top left quadrant downwards to the bottom left quadrant of *unconscious bicultural competence*. On this quadrant I was effectively 'asleep', the living dead, making choices blindly and compulsively in order to survive, despite the numerous contradictions experienced. The existential crisis of meaning referred to earlier woke me out of deep sleep compelling me to respond at last to the 'call to adventure' (Campbell, 2003) in terms of examining the 'black experience' – a call I had always ignored before. This acceptance of the call placed me firmly but belatedly on the quadrant of *conscious bicultural incompetence* and the journey of self-re-education/authentic human development.

	Unconscious	Conscious
Bicultural Incompetence	don't know/don't know (dk/dk) (nurturing)	Know/don't know (k/dk) (self-re-education)
Bicultural Competence	don't know/know (dk/k) (asleep)	Know/know (k/k) (choice/awareness)
	Think I know but don't know (tk/dk) (learned ignoramus)	Know/pretend don't know (k/pdk) (social actor)

Figure 4 – Bicultural Competence Matrix

The requirement for bicultural awareness is based on the existence of two or more competing or oppositional forces, as seen in black and white cultures in Britain. When I started my PhD studies my focus in terms of bicultural competence had been on the black and white experiences. Post PhD, the bicultural imperative in my own work is now focused on harmonising inner and outer realities. Channing points to the deeper significance of slavery when he notes (Armistead, 1848:39):

> The moral influence of Slavery is to destroy the proper consciousness and spirit of a Man. The Slave, regarded and treated as property, bought and sold like a brute, denied the rights of humanity, unprotected against insult, made a tool, and systematically subdued, that he may be a manageable, useful tool, how can he help regarding himself as fallen below his race? How must his spirit be crushed? How can he respect himself? He becomes bowed to servility. This word, borrowed from his condition, expresses the ruin wrought by Slavery within him. The idea that he was made for his own virtue and happiness scarcely dawns on his mind. To be an instrument of the physical material good of another, whose will is his highest law, he is taught to regard as the great purpose of being. The whips and imprisonment of Slavery, and even the horrors of the middle passage from Africa to America, these are not to be named in comparison with this extinction of the proper consciousness of a human being, with the degradation of a man into a brute.

> It may be said that the Slave is used to his yoke; that his sensibilities are blunted; that he receives, without a pang or a thought, the treatment which would sting other men to madness. And to what does this apology amount? It virtually declares, that Slavery has done its perfect work, has quenched the

spirit of humanity, that the Man is dead within the Slave. It is not, however, true that this work of abasement is ever so effectually done as to extinguish all feeling. *Man is too great a creature to be wholly ruined by Man. When he seems dead he only sleeps.* There are occasionally some sullen murmurs in the calm of Slavery, showing that life still beats in the soul, that the idea of Rights cannot be wholly effaced from the human being...

I now understood that there is a significant inner life that needs nourishing but which black culture, signifying enforced unconsciousness, is not equipped to do. It was necessary for me to awaken from the sleep into which being a DoEA, slavery had thrown me to do the work on myself that would bring about the outcomes depicted in figure 5 below.

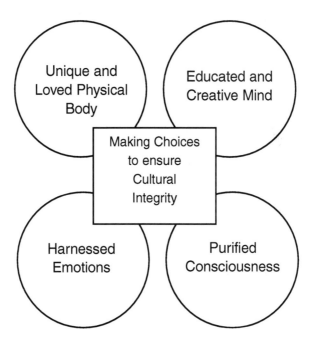

Figure 5 – The rehumanised British African-Caribbean

This re-humanised British African-Caribbean (BAC) perspective is based on a new psychological contract with myself, knowledge (historical, ethnic, cultural, emotional, spiritual, mental/psychological) and being an autodidactic learner. I am a work in process. Re-humanisation means 'casting a new shadow' and thus has heralded many changes in both my personal and professional life; too much for a short chapter like this. The surfacing of these findings is timely given the challenges of globalisation with which we are all now grappling. For me it is significant that these findings should come from a member of the group that was the primary focus of the first phase of globalisation: enslaved Africans and their descendants. It seems we are at a time in human history when the memes of DoEAs (BAC) has become important and is now needed.

Where am I now

Twelve years after completing my PhD I continue to work as a lecturer in the Business, Computing and Information Management Faculty of London South Bank University in the Human Resources and Management Department. I am today a National Teaching Fellow (NTF), a direct outcome of changes due to my awakening from the long sleep of slavery. I continue to strive for cultural integrity as a BAC in a society which does not necessarily recognise me as such on account of our shared history. I have liberated my voice to the point I now share my understanding of race as a BAC – not as a 'black'. I continue to have to find ways in which to couch my findings and choices as a means of not triggering the racialised emotions of the white ethnic majority. It seems that all of my silences have been necessary to protect the comfort zones of white significant others, in a bid for my own self-protection. Self-definition as a BAC has liberated me in that I can now speak from an informed place across cultures. It is now apparent that cross-cultural dialogue does not take place between blacks and whites in British culture – rather black and white cultures routinise and perpetuate the oppositional black-white duality.

In my own case continual engagement with the process of authentic human development has supported the emergence of a self at the elder stage of the life cycle. This has coincided with my arriving at the elder stage in terms of chronological age. Post-PhD, I engage experientially in learning what it means to be an elder as a DoEA, given that enforced black socialisation does not facilitate eldership development. These years have been particularly challenging as I have been learning the art and skill of negotiation across oppositional cultures.

In 2007 my book, *Towards Bicultural Competence: Beyond Black and White* became the published testimony to my ongoing human inquiry. The critical insight brought forward from my PhD studies is that knowledge is not applied to the life experience of DoEAs. Instead we are the victims of grafted knowledge (Akbar, 1995) keeping us locked into a dependent relationship with the ethnic majority (SCMH, 2002) at the adolescent stage of the life cycle as a group. In this position we are not equipped to take responsibility for our own lives. In terms of ongoing research my understanding of these issues challenges me to take on the responsibility of developing knowledge that facilitates choice and thereby power for DoEAs, and doing this in a way that explicitly integrates theory with practice. The new learning age we are currently in is rich with opportunities for DoEAs – if they can be reached – because of the focus on self-discovery and self-mastery. The structural embeddedness of black and white cultures within British culture means, however, that initiatives such as Widening Participation, Aiming High, etc are designed to fail as long as they are transmitting a message of black dysfunctionality.

I also founded the Centre for British African Caribbean Studies (CBACS) at London South Bank University in 2007. CBACS returns human studies to the centre of the curriculum, signifying the integrative cultural work which must be achieved not just by DoEAs but by all of us, in order to harmonise our own inner community of self (Akbar, 1985). This harmonised community of self is a pre-requisite for achieving a harmonised external community and world. CBACS facilitates this process of transformation and self-renewal for those who want to achieve this kind of breakthrough in their lives by offering not just 'informative' but also 'formative' education. To facilitate this process The *Metanoia* Project 2007-2034, with its two strands (BAC) and (Teach), was also launched in 2007. More recently the work of CBACS has been consolidated under the umbrella of The Global Leaders for Tomorrow programme.

Human Centred Passionate Appreciation/Meta-Cultural Competence

Self knowledge is not a self indulgent or narcissistic pursuit but instead essential to dispelling the illusions and confusions which we all learn, and which lead us down the wrong paths. As I have related here, my educational ideas did not develop through academic efforts made in the quiet and relative leisure of the study. Rather, they were born of the back-and-forth interplay between theory and practice under a multitude of pressures. I struggled against constraining circumstances, fear and white authority figures even as I grappled with the question of how best to establish a firm foundation for the life-long happiness of learners in my classrooms. I was seeking to develop a teaching and learning philosophy fit for all the children of the world.

Is it possible to love all peoples beyond the normalised problematisation of difference? I have inductively devised a teaching and learning strategy which says yes we can. We can do this by choosing to see every individual as a complex five-dimensional human being engaged in the human task of being creators of culture (Gordon, 2007). This is not, however, a task that everyone realises they are engaged in because human studies is not a standard component of the education process. This is, I came to realise, the missing part of the jigsaw that I was looking for when I found myself in an existential crisis of meaning in the early 1980s. Taking a second look at Figure 1 we can see that focus is placed almost exclusively, and negatively when black, on the physical – with the other four dimensions largely eclipsed, at least in the black experience. This was the source of all my problems. I was not conscious of my own choices because I lacked self-knowledge. Important underpinning assumptions of the HCPA educational philosophy, the 'human centred turn', developed so as to ensure learners achieve the human task of becoming conscious creators of culture. This includes facilitating learners in:

- Learning about and reflecting comprehensively on what it means to be *a whole fully alive experiencing choiceful human being* based on Gordon's (2007) five dimensional human being model resulting in whole people in a whole world

- *Personalising education* to meet the needs of individual learners

- Developing the *conscious bicultural competence* (Gordon, 2007) of learners, enabling them to effectively achieve the human task of being conscious creators of culture

- ▩ Using *transformational and self-renewal approaches* designed to liberate learner potential

- ▩ Engaging in *human rights education* as a means of preventing further human rights violations and as a vital component of the democratic process

- ▩ Developing *'passionate appreciation'* as a life choice, relational ideal and as a means of protecting the emotional and spiritual well-being of learners

- ▩ Understanding the responsibility of being *champions of important human values* like 'freedom'

- ▩ Development of 'eldership' identity (based on life cycle) embedding ideals of personal and social responsibility

- ▩ Making a service contribution based on one's own unique 'personal factor' (identity capital)

The HCPA philosophy is not new. It consists of what is commonsense and ethical when it comes to the human experience. It has been developed as a compensatory model for what has been missing in not just my own life, but in that of my children's and students' education as black members of British society. It is also what I see still missing in the education system today. I teach subject content in the context of a learning environment which nourishes these outcomes in learners. It is a demanding process but allows me to bring my unique personal factor into the world. In the process I have learned that the world in which we live is our own creation – but somewhere along the line we have lost that awareness. It is time for us to retrieve what has been lost. This is particularly true for those of us who are DoEAs. Back in 1956 Mumford stated:

> Man's principal task today is to create a new self, adequate to command the forces that operate so aimlessly and yet so compulsively ... Such a culture must be nourished, not only by a new vision of the whole, but a new vision of self capable of understanding and cooperating with the whole. In short the moment for another great historic transformation has come. (p1)

Concluding thoughts

My own research journey has taught me that the forces Mumford refers to are within ourselves, as seen in the four invisible and unintegrated dimensions of mind, emotions, spirit and culture. These are aspects of the human makeup which go largely unattended as the focus is placed on physical differences. I now understand that psychological slavery is a state of consciousness from which we can move if we have appropriate facilitation. The most significant challenges preventing this movement for 'black people' from happening in contemporary society are several. First is the institutionalisation of the black and white identifiers as used and perpetuated by government policy. Second is the strength of the black-white duality – a cultural force – kept in place consciously and unconsciously by the dynamic reciprocal role relating behaviours enacted between blacks and whites on a moment by moment basis in our everyday lives. And third is the drive for power, underpinned by greed, which has resulted in what Bales (1999) refers to as the 'new slavery' of the invisible global economy. If slavery – the imposition of limitation on the human spirit – is to be eradicated from the human experience then education that meets the needs of conscious bicultural in/competence is now vital. The global crisis we are currently experiencing is not essentially technical or economic but cultural and spiritual. Culture, the human task, is the very ground of our being. Globalisation, it seems, is presenting us with the challenge of finding a metaculture that unites us as a human family beyond physical differences. I particularly like MacIntosh's (1989:2) definition of metaculture:

> ... the transcultural foundation of culture: that which gives meaning not just because we have a particular language, customs, art, religion and metaphysic, but, simply yet profoundly *because we are human beings*. Like islands in the sea, one culture may appear unconnected to another when viewed superficially across the water. But in reality they are one at foundation level – through the rock; the metaculture.

5

Dusting off my doctorate

Helen M Gunter

Introduction

A colleague who is doing a doctorate recently gave me a copy of Caroline Steedman's (2001) book, *Dust*, about our relationship with archives. One of the most thought provoking books I have read in a long time, it helped me to think my way into this chapter:

> This is what Dust is about; this is what Dust is: what it means and what it is. It is not about rubbish, nor about the discarded; it is not about a surplus, left over from something else; it is not about Waste. Indeed, Dust is the opposite thing to Waste, or at least, the opposite principle to Waste. It is about circularity, the impossibility of things disappearing, or going away, or being gone. Nothing can be destroyed. (p164)

In taking my bound PhD thesis from 1999 off the shelf and turning the pages I am not just removing the dust from everyday living, I am going into something that is alive and central to who I am and who others close to me are (Gunter, 1999). In looking at the blue cover, the gold lettering, the crisp white pages, the text with letters and numbers in a particular order, I can see not only an account of something that I spent five years of my life thinking and writing about, but also that there is a history here of my life.

What looks to be linear, neat and tidy was messy, crazy and wonderfully exciting. The thesis is an archived moment that says so much more to me as I have memories about the life in which this thesis happened: I typed, I wrote with pen and paper, I talked, I thought, I cried, I drank coffee, I read, I listened, I was silent, I slept and I wept. While the pages are themselves intrinsically silent, there is a noisy biography within it, and my construction of this narrative is clearly based on self-authoring in the here and now. Notably my post postgraduate experiences are an important lens through which I have emplotted this 'history-in-person' (Holland and Lave, 2001:5-6), not least how the thesis has shaped my ongoing research project. There is no autobiographical revelation of who I am or why I am as I am, but instead it is a narrative about dust that in looking back from now means something about how I now understood then.

A sense of place

At some point in the last fifty years I have come to learn that libraries are the place where I feel most at ease. I don't know when it happened. But thinking about this chapter has generated this realisation. I recall that going into the new library built in the early 1970s in the town where I grew up was exciting because the building seemed so large, with space to browse between the shelves without bumping into each other. Some- how I didn't feel that I belonged. I found reading difficult, and while I read the *Famous Five* and *Secret Seven* books when I was twelvish I don't think I actually read fiction for pleasure until I was an adult.

One of my fellow students on the teacher training course (1979-1980, so I was 22) told me about Tom Sharpe's books, such as *Wilt*, and I bought one and read it and laughed so much I bought another one. I had clearly been a slow learner (I read *Bimbo* as a child up to the age of eight or nine when most of my friends had moved over to *Bunty*). For most of my early life I didn't really know what to do with reading, what it was meant to do, to make you feel like or how it was meant to make a difference. I didn't understand what interpretation meant, and how to bridge what I read into the world in which I lived. I loved TV and the cinema, and I would watch dramas and films for hours on end (particularly Bette Davis films), and so I understood narrative and character, but it was visual and oral, and reading was difficult. I could read, as I read books in class, but I don't think I could actually read in the sense of fully grasp- ing meaning and that I could interpret what I read and use my imagina- tion. I had grown up in a world of common sense and so other worlds in books did not speak to me for a long time.

When I walked into the library at Liverpool University in 1976 I immediately loved the smell of books. It felt normal and enabling. I had taken my time to go into that building as I had grown up in a schooling culture where you shouldn't show that you are keen to learn and do your work. Once in the library where I saw all these people reading in silence I realised that this is the world that I had wanted to be a part of, but up until that time I had not been able to admit to it, to myself or to others. From then on I spent my life in the library and breathed in the dust of past writing and thinking. I accepted it for what is seemed to be, the repository of research and knowledge that people older, wiser, normally male and more powerful than me had written, and they were often dead and so I had to respect their lives and work. I experienced the library as a rational place with order (vertical and horizontal shelving) and classification (numbers and letters on spines), where I translated reading lists into reality by bringing the factory disposition of my family and community's working lives into the University. Interestingly, I experienced new structuring process, because increasingly I learned to move from the reading lists to explore for new and interesting texts that I had not been directed to read but which seemed interesting.

One such journey led me to find the letters between the last Tsar and Tsarina of Russia, and what an encounter that was. On the eve of the revolution they were talking with each other as if all was normal, and I learned more about the Russian Revolutions of 1917 from those letters than from all the historical accounts I had read. I did need to take care though I once discovered at the end of one of my rummages in the library that while I had a pile of books to take out, my library card was in my handbag which I had left somewhere on a shelf. What had been an unplanned journey in search of exotic ideas now had to have a *post hoc* rationalisation, as I tried to recount my steps through the stacks to recover my bag. I did find it but the episode made me more aware of the need to keep my wits about me when bathing in books.

In taking forward the PhD from 1994 I learned so much more about libraries and how the dust settles in the volumes and the ideas. My thesis came to illustrate for me that much of the dust created by my own field was not being studied or examined. So I took some ideas to a colleague, and from this my thesis emerged over the next five years. I set out to study the field of educational management, a field that I had been unwittingly a member of for many years. I had been a teacher in an 11-18 comprehensive school, from the time I completed my PGCE in 1980 till 1991, and then moved into higher education where, as a lecturer, I not only practiced management but I studied it as well. Reading the journals and books, and attending conferences gave me entrance into the ideas, the methods and the writers, who I met and conversed with. It seemed to me that the question I had asked myself while a school teacher when I started my part time MSc in Educational Management in 1987 was still valid: where has all this stuff on management come from and why is it being brought into education? I was studying this at a momentous time because the 1988 Education Reform Act brought about site based management with schools being turned into small businesses, and I wanted to know why models and thinking from research into private companies had higher status than education.

I took this forward in my PhD by reading the articles and books, and by interviewing the people who had brought educational management into higher education as an area of legitimate study and professional practice. I undertook an intellectual history of the field through a study of people and their work, and I loved every minute of it. In retrospect it seems that my factory disposition had undergone some restructuring into one of activism and creativity. What I learned through this work is that the library I had entered in a respectful and deferential way as an undergraduate in 1976 is a power structure. I entered the library at Keele University in 1994 as a doctoral student, someone who now recognised that there are knowers who have particular forms of knowing and use libraries and other powerful means to promote sacred knowledge. Citations between people in particular epistemic groups has continued to be a fascination for me. What I learned through using Bourdieu's ideas is that knowledge production is a struggle over what is to be known, who by and in whose interests. The veil fell from my eyes, and the journey through the book stacks containing the ideas of others became a journey to develop my own ideas and thinking. After I had graduated in 1999 *Pascalian Meditations* was published in English (Bourdieu, 2000), and in it Bourdieu identifies the 'scholastic illusion' where, through writing and referencing, particular writers and texts are canonised as forms of 'ritual embalming' (p48). Clearly I did this too during my undergraduate and masters work, but it was the PhD that liberated me. Here I could chart and understand the field and begin to grasp the place I wanted to have within it. In other words, the library and its dust could be rearranged by myself and I could give meaning to the archive in ways that are scholarly, legitimate and meaningful. So I could join the dusty shelves.

Girls like me don't do PhDs

My first degree is in modern history and politics (1976-1979), and there are two episodes that at the time shocked me, although I carried on regardless with my reading and essay writing. I recall a history professor asking the seminar group what the picture on the front cover of a book on the working classes showed. I saw an overweight woman behind a fruit and vegetable stall, wearing a woolly hat and a huge woolly cardigan. She had a careworn face. There was little response from the group, and he then pronounced that she was the face of the working class woman. While I recognised this face, it did not speak to me of all working class women. My mother would not have allowed such a picture of her to have been taken. My mother, and the women who lived on the public housing estate where I lived, would not dress like that or show such a lack of care about their appearance.

What this professor did not understand is the importance of wearing your Sunday best and being seen to be respectable. Putting a milk bottle on the kitchen table was just not acceptable in our house. My grandmother grew up on the same street as a famous trade union leader, but his family were looked down on because the front door step was never washed (or 'donkey stoned' into a bright white colour). The professor did not understand that the working class is not one homogenous group but is highly differentiated, with issues of status that are constantly visible and open to applause or condemnation. My shock was how I was unable to defend my class and sex, particularly through how the power to know in an authoritative way was presented to me by the professor. I didn't have the confidence or the language to do it – my first language is Lancashire dialect – so silence, so necessary in a library, was my response.

I guess this has a link with my second story. During my first degree I read Ralph Miliband's *The State in Capitalist Society* (1973). In a footnote he reports research evidence by Little and Westergaard that states '...an unskilled manual worker's daughter has a chance of only one in five or six hundred of entering a university – a chance in a hundred times lower than if she had been born into a professional family' (p39). There in front of me was the evidence about my situation. I was a rarity, and I took refuge in the library because I did not have to account for myself there.

The silence helped me to cope with being odd. For example, people asked me about having a good weekend, but I really did not understand this. My weekends were for housework, gardening and church, interspersed with TV and films. I had experience of an annual holiday to Blackpool, and treats of going on a saloon for a day out on a Saturday or by train to Liverpool to see a new film, usually historical, but beyond that our finances meant that we could not stray. Poverty stops you thinking about possibilities.

Parents who don't earn very much make sacrifices for their children. In the early 1970s (I must have been about 13 or 14) I went to stay with my pen friend in Athens for a month, and what an adventure that was! My parents saved hard and did without to pay for this. The experience of spending even such a short time in a country led by a military junta, where there was no free speech and the fear of arrest, impacted enormously on my identity. I came back not only wanting to eat food we couldn't afford, but also having experienced totalitarianism first hand. This continues to affect my life and work, and made me realise how liberty to speak and to think are integral to civilised society.

This reflexive journey has helped me to see that I found certain types of oral communication difficult, but when you speak you must be clear and direct. Having come from a town where the majority of the population worked in the coal mine or the factory, I was used to straight talking: talk when you need to, mean what you say and be clear, no ambiguity. I have come to realise that this is because people lived their lives in ways that were endemically vulnerable. Working arrangements (coal mining, foundry, mill) were not conducive to everyday conversation. Talking while you work had to have a purpose, and if you did not speak clearly someone might die. I recall my mother telling me the story of how she worked in the weaving shed, tending multiple looms at once, and how one of the foremen bent down to pick something up and as he got up the arm that moved rapidly backwards and forwards to send the shuttle with the weft through the warp hit him on the temple. Dead. People in their everyday lives chatted and gossiped, and debated politics in their preciously short break time, but their working communication always had to be mindful of being literal and clear. I might not say much but when I do you get it straight.

Alan Bennett (1994) has helped me to understand the wonders of working class lives, and how people are categorised. He recalls how 'my mother's scheme of things admitted to much finer distinctions than were allowed by the sociologists. She'd talk about people being 'better class', 'well-off', 'nicely spoken', 'refined', 'educated', 'genuine', 'ordinary' and the ultimate condemnation – 'common'' (p43-44). This is exactly my experience, and to witness women being declared common by the women I worked with on the checkouts at Asda when I was a sixth form and university student (1974-1979) was a lesson in how shame operated.

I don't know where people learned to look disapprovingly at others who had been identified as having to be shamed, but there seemed to be an angle to the head, with the use of staring eyes, and a whispered comment sideways to another (you never walked around at work on your own, always in pairs or a group). However, not fitting in by going to university (I was the first in the family and the second in the street to go) was not categorised as shameful. I was in receipt of the odd 'who does she think she is' type of comment, but in the main people where supportive I was doing something that they quietly hoped their kids might do.

I was once on the checkouts at Asda in the summer break, alongside a fellow student who was doing a PhD in physiology. I was stunned that girls like me might do a PhD and I remember this, putting it into my memory 'bank' of girls who had broken through – though I once stacked shelves with a girl my age who wanted to be a mortician, and while impressed that someone had an ambition to do this, it was not a career goal for me.

Going to university brought me into contact with the middle classes, who talked in ways that I did not understand, and still find challenging. Fitting in and feeling shame when you don't does not seem to feature in their lives. In higher education most decisions are unlikely to be life and death ones, and so communication can be used to attack people rather than to get the job done and care about or for people. Being in meetings where people argue for something they don't themselves want but do want to stop someone else having is something I find bizarre. It is such a waste of energy and ideas and talent. I came to realise that there is a middle class form of being common. It is about rampant individualism, so beloved by Mrs Thatcher, who denied altruism and the basic human capacity to care for and about others outside of the family.

Being a girl with a womb and boobs, or realising that not having testicles matters in the world, does come into my reflections on how I have begun to understand the place of the PhD in my life. In doing so I am mindful of Steedman's (2005) analysis that 'working-class childhood is problematic because of the many ways in which it has been pathologised over the last century' (p127), not least through how such a life is assumed to be in deficit without the richness of economic and cultural capital. The current label of 'disadvantaged children' is one that my parents would be ashamed to have associated with our family. We may not have had a lot of money but we were not disadvantaged. The people we saw on TV in middle class situation comedies or dramas may have had expensive clothes and holidays, but they did not always have love and care.

Steedman (2005) talks about the 'feeling of childhood' where 'memory alone cannot resurrect past time, because it is memory itself that shapes it, long after historical time has passed' (p29). I don't remember consciously learning that girls are to be girls and to do girl type things, but there are memorable events that I do recall. Being a good girl by doing as you are told, being modest and passive, and receiving praise from adults for being a good girl was all that seemed to matter for such a long time. Conformity in language, dress and actions are key, and I think I share this disposition with the other authors in this collection. It was there in everyday social practice, and if you stepped out of line then the usual comment was 'that's not very ladylike' and the last thing you wanted was to be labelled common as that would be damnation. It was deep in the curriculum, with Janet and John books extolling the virtues of Janet helping mummy as a good girl. I was expected to finish school, get a job for a while, be courted by a nice boy, get married, have children, bring them up to be good – or at least not common – and die ... without the shame of debt.

As a Catholic I might do the seriously good girl thing and become a nun, and so bring acclaim to the family – though not as great a celebration as for a boy becoming a priest. But this was not for me. When I moved from *Bunty* to *Jackie*, the seriously delicious David Cassidy came into my life – school life was divided into David Cassidy and Donny Osmond fans. At late primary and early secondary school I was going to be a hairdresser, and I did my doll's hair in wondrous styles that received much praise. Vanessa and her blonde hair would be sculptured in the styles of the day, and if you watch the 1960s TV series *The Champions* then you would be familar with the style I could do that copied the character of Sharron Macready played by Alexandra Bastedo.

I guess it was from such characters – along with Diana Rigg in *The Avengers* – that I learned that women could take safe risks. They can do important and challenging jobs as long as they are well groomed with neat hair, and men could be gentlemen and protect them. We watched *The Brothers* every Sunday evening, and while the hair styles were not particularly interesting, it is clear that one of the wives drank too much (like Su Ellen in *Dallas*), largely because she had been let down by a man – moral of the story is get a solid man, and if you don't then you shouldn't moan about it because 'thas made tha bed, tha mun lie in it' which translates as 'you have made your bed, you must lie in it' or you have made choices and you have to live with them. On the other hand, one of the secretaries or PA, as I came to understand her role, was a good girl in a good job: she did the job for the chief executive, and my mum once said that women in such jobs can do important work in helping the man make decisions and run the company. Wow! I realised I might be able to do something other than hairdressing because a man might let me do it.

All of this was at the time of the sexual revolution. But I remember my mum, when we were discussing doing teaching, saying that now that women get equal pay they will have to teach the demanding kids, the big boys whom previously only men taught and consequently got more money. Where did she learn this, and how did I break out of it in ways that meant I could still officially be a good girl?

In recounting my agency – and lack of it at times – in this story I associate with Deem's (1996) analysis that, like her career, the stories I tell about my life are 'neither a unified entity nor a series of carefully planned, rational, measured steps. What had occurred has frequently been contingent, rarely linear, sometimes accidental and often serendipitous' (p6).

After eleven years of teaching I found myself a senior lecturer at Leeds Polytechnic in 1991, where I was asked to write a module on gender and management for the MSc in Education Management programme I had been appointed to teach on. So I began reading and my world changed. I read papers and books on gender, on the social construction of practice, and importantly that biology does not determine practice. Women don't manage or lead in a particular way because they have a womb, but they may operate in a particular way because they are expected to. From this I was beginning to grasp the interplay between agency and structure that later in that decade would become a key feature of my reading, through what was to become a life long association with Bourdieu's theory of practice.

What is important to acknowledge here is that: '...the historical conditions under which we operate and the events and contexts in which we find ourselves situated or participating are central to an understanding of the life-course trajectory of any individual' (Deem, 1996:6). I had been brought up by parents who had lost their youth and the idea of fun to the war effort. On returning to peace they had rationing and hard work in the home and factory. What they wanted was security to raise a family in the best way they could. In their shoes I think I would have wanted the same. At the time of massive change in the sixties it was too late to recover the excitement eclipsed by 1939. They had settled into their lives, and had settled myself and my brother into the right sort of dispositions to enable secure futures.

My future was mapped out early, as I failed the 11+ so in 1969 I went to a secondary modern school. There I learned the basics, and was being prepared to be a socially acceptable working class girl through a vocational curriculum of home economics, needlework and typing. The map was redrawn in two ways: first, I was in the first year of the Raising of the School Leaving Age (ROSLA) in 1972 so I had to stay on to the age of sixteen, and second, the biggest impact on my life was comprehensive education. Previously the system had told my generation that we were failures at eleven and I recall that I had a conscious decision to prove to the world that I am not thick. The disposition that led to the PhD was clearly structured here. When I was thirteen years old the revolution to the system through comprehensivisation told my generation that we were now worth investing in and that we could do the same things as the grammar school kids. Not least because the 11+ had been shown to have class bias in how it worked, and while some working class kids did do well out of it – two out of my primary school class of 30 went to grammar school – the rest faced a different curriculum and future.

Comprehensive education brought new buildings, new teachers, a new curriculum, and a sixth form. I did both CSEs and O-levels at sixteen, as the early days saw a policy of entering everyone for CSE and a few were double entered for O-levels. I had learned to touch type (a wonderful skill that I am deeply grateful for) but also to access an academic curriculum. The lack of Latin remains an issue but I have incrementally filled in the gaps. The new teachers had degrees, and some of them were women, and with a new sixth form with A-levels I had another option in life. The teachers talked of going to university and so for the first time this was an option in ways it had not been for my brother, who is five years older and had to wait until he was much older to do a part time Open University degree. So I stayed on at school, got A levels and applied to University.

What do I know anyway?

The ideas for a PhD that I took to my colleague, Professor Jenny Ozga in 1994 were around issues of gender and also of a field. The decision to study the field of educational management and the supervisions sessions over five years remain important spaces for me, where I learned to be a social science researcher. I remain deeply indebted to Jenny's generosity and how she enabled my very tentative ideas and thinking to grow into a project that I am still working on. I can say this with some confidence because at a research training session on a Saturday morning at Keele University, someone told the group of postgraduate students that we would never actually finish our projects; we would just stop when the thesis was ready to be examined. This not only took the burden off my shoulders, because I already thought I would never actually finish the study, it also gave me permission to see the research as a productive career trajectory.

The project is about knowledge production in the field of educational management, and the interviews I did with people who brought the field into higher education and also the reading of the books, articles, conference papers in the field have enabled me to gain an understanding of the production of dust and its circularity (Gunter, 1999). More recently I have completed an extension of this work through studying New Labour policy and the leadership of schools, and this has widened the pool of interviewees to include not only researchers in higher education but also policymakers and practitioners (Gunter and Forrester, 2008). What has been crucial has been the realisation that research gives a person the right to speak in new and interesting ways. And the originality of the topic and the depth of knowledge of the PhD has enabled me to gain understandings that are particular to myself. This is a major shift. While comprehensive education helped me to gain access to a fairer education system and then a degree helped me to gain access to an academic education, the PhD helped me to know and understand not only my field but my place in relation to it.

The PhD also confirmed my identity as a writer. While as a lecturer driven by the Research Assessment Excercise I had written some journal articles, and while writing the thesis I wrote a book (Gunter, 1997), it has been post thesis that the avalanche of writing has taken place. While I had struggled with books for much of my childhood, I had not had problems with writing. This seems bizarre to me, as I had not been formally trained in grammatical rules, but I had picked it up somewhere and somehow. I recall doing O-level Spanish at secondary school and the teacher talking about syllables and consonants, and I didn't have a clue what this meant.

The PhD has been and remains the longest piece of sustained and complete writing I have done. My obsession with hairdressing has been transferred to word processing; writing is central to who I am and my purpose in the world. What the PhD did was to help me learn how to build an argument and edit, because it would come under scrutiny through the viva. I had to take control of my writing in ways that Ball describes (Carnell *et al*, 2008), and I had to meet my insecurities head on and think not only about what I was writing but the tone and nuanced nature of it. The word processor and all the software were so important to me, and helped me in ways that the typewriter I used in my first degree assignments could not. The ability to draft and redraft, to cut and paste is so important. My mantra continues to be to write it and *then* get it right.

I could have undertaken a doctoral study that is within the field, such as a study of headteachers, or teachers, or gender, or the curriculum. However, I did a PhD thesis on the field itself. I sought to understand the purposes and practices of the field, what professional practice was in the field and why, and what the field thought of other fields in education. I read across field boundaries, so I read not only the mainstream management texts but also texts on school improvement and effectiveness, as well as on policy sociology. Like Deem (1996), I have done and continue to do a lot of border crossing and for this I can be sidelined as I don't fit, but I do not see this as a problem:

> This blurring, shifting and reforming of borders has enabled the establishment of new areas of work, the formulation of novel approaches and the creation of fresh ideas. Living in border territory, belonging neither to one camp nor the other, can enhance the willingness to take intellectual risks and permits an open-ness to new ideas that may be less characteristic of those who live within more defined and more central academic areas. (p16)

However, while the creativity is evident in such positioning it is also, as Bourdieu (1988) identifies, dangerous. Behind the scenes attacks began on me before I did the PhD and during the process I wrote a book (Gunter, 1997) and they stopped for a while. There are clear attempts to bully my scholarship out of the field, but I am not the only person to experience this (see Greenfield and Ribbins, 1992). How others have coped has been an inspiration. There seems to be a culture within the field of what Greenfield (1978) called 'the tidy minded' (p90) where there is little understanding that fields are spaces for the debate of ideas. The PhD meant that silence had ended for me, but a serious consequence has been that there are those who do not want things to be said and so behave in unscholarly and illiberal ways.

However, intellectual work cannot be silenced – history shows that. Thinking and writing I have done with Tanya Fitzgerald (Fitzgerald and Gunter, 2005; Gunter and Fitzgerald, 2007) asks questions about whose knowledge counts and why? We juxtaposed centre and periphery, and identified that while as professors we might be seen to be included and powerful, as women who work on issues of social justice we might be excluded. As a school teacher I had been told by a senior manager in school that I would never get on in education because I didn't have children, and so the equal opportunities law did not protect me. As an academic I was told by a senior colleague that my work on knowledge production would never get funded. Two years later I won an ESRC project, but at another university.

Keeping the promise of the PhD alive through continued research and thinking is central to my ongoing project, and by continuing to cross borders, map territory, and bring back news of ideas and thinking, my voice will hopefully remain loud and clear. This has emerged as a double edged project: it is scholarly through research and thinking, but it is also a social practice in demonstrating that in spite of the bullying and harassment from within higher education I can continue to be productive, and smile.

Central to my ability to do this has been my association with great colleagues, including Professors Tanya Fitzgerald, Peter Ribbins, and Pat Thomson. With Peter I have undertaken some important work on mapping the field that grew directly out of my PhD research (Gunter and Ribbins, 2003). With both Tanya and Pat I have worked on developing critical analysis and developing alternatives for the field, and this has been through work on leadership (Fitzgerald and Gunter, 2009) and student voice (Thomson and Gunter, 2006). This has truly enriched my world, not just because it is fun with fun people, but also because it is with scholarly people who put the integrity of data and thinking at the top of their agendas. This is where I feel comfortable, working with people who read the literatures, generate ideas and thinking, and from this develop project ideas and publications that are directly concerned with real lives. I think this is because the PhD had taken five years of my life and continues to live within my practice, and so like all doctoral studies it was tough, and quite rightly so. Hence I find it difficult to operate in a world teeming with power-pointed presentations. I have written about this before (Gunter and Willmott, 2002). The over use of bullet points is for me like an embalming fluid. The onscreen presentation may looks swish but there is little actual thinking going on. This may sound harsh but my field is full of 'how to do it' ringbinders containing solutions which are given to people who have been told that they are the problem that must be solved.

It could be argued that Bourdieu's theory of practice is miserable because although his thinking tools of field and habitus help to understand the situation a person is in, it does not help to get them out of it. I had to address this issue in my thesis, because I had charted and analysed a field using Bourdieu's thinking tools so needed to assess how helpful this had been. What his work did for me and continues to do is to help those who work in fields of knowledge production to ask: who sets the agenda? Is the research agenda a given on the basis of government priorities? I find this very pessimistic. Might researchers in universities recognise that academics are not the servants of other people's agendas but that they can develop alternative ideas and thinking? What doctoral work does is to help a person understand that they are not solely responsible for the world they inhabit or the problems that are encountered in everyday practice. This is not irresponsible – it is the recognition that the world is created and recreated every day and that things can be done differently by the self and with others.

What is needed is a form of reflexivity that enables the researcher to understand how domination can be challenged. This is through understanding how what is 'normal' is what Bourdieu and Wacquant (1992) call 'misrecognition' identified as 'the fact of recognising a violence which is wielded precisely inasmuch as one does not perceive it as such' (p168). Thinking about and studying the underlying knowledge claims of a field can enable a knowledge worker such as myself to challenge the established truths so that purposes and practices are open to review and development in ways that are scholarly. Doing the research and writing a thesis that is called a PhD helped me to see that silence is not an option, and that when I speak orally and in writing, I must speak also about the claims about the truths and not just assume that a truth can float free of me and my epistemology. A PhD can be the process through which a person is co-opted into a regime of domination, but for me it was the arena through which I learned to understand the process of domination.

Out of darkness cometh light

One of the things I have not talked about is my private life. I don't have any hang-ups about this; it is just that my PhD and my private life did not collide. Barry is and will always be the love of my life. The PhD was for a while the third person in our relationship, as it took me away from time we might spend together, and it meant that I always had reason to be on the computer. But it also gave him the opportunity to return to the football with a season ticket for Wolverhampton Wanderers Football Club. An expensive PhD, I hear you say. But the Wolves' motto, as the final section heading, is appropriate. What the PhD did for me is help me to see with more clarity who I am and the type of life I enjoy living. I had a happy and secure childhood. Others decided that I needed a better chance at education, and being given access to it through comprehensive education made me want more. Those who had argued for and continue to argue for comprehensive education achieved a wonderful development. This is dust that has been officially declared under New Labour as bog standard, and from the position of being a beneficiary of a comprehensive school and having taught in one, I can declare that there is nothing bog standard about it. Thousands of kids stopped being written off at the age of eleven and the school could be the place for the creation of a stable and emerging democratic experience.

Social mobility is less of an opportunity now because of Thatcher and her regime of individualism based on logos and competitive schooling. Disappointingly, it was continued by New Labour. The opportunities for a universal education system are no more, the changes in the past decade have been built on the fabrication of consumer choice. I had the choice to go to university, and to do a part time masters and PhD, because society supported and invested in me and people like me. The chances I had have now gone: choice is now an economic rather than a social process. The world has turned back to the 1930s, a time when my parents could not have gone to university because the education system and the economy excluded it from their imagined futures. Comprehensive education was a moment in time when all children at eleven could go to the same school, learn and mix together, and be successful in lots of different ways, together. Now kids have to rely on philanthropy for investment in an academy rather than on their community to fund their education as a public good. I could not have gone to university now – the cost and the looming debt would have made it impossible. Getting into debt is what common people do (what my upbringing has taught me to call the feckless poor, but even the new class of feckless rich who have brought our economy to the brink of collapse can now be incorporated into this shaming, and shameful, paradigm).

So central to my intellectual and ongoing project is to keep alive history and how the world could be different. While this is inconvenient to the neoliberals and their gurus, it is vital that I stay hopeful and try to keep the spaces open for alternative ways of living in the world. As others have shown more clearly than myself, the public realm is in danger, and for me religious community is not the way to create a sense of the social. Religion is divisive and delusionary. I would much rather put my faith in humans, and the situation that needs attention has been well described by Arendt (2000):

> The point then is not that there is a lack of public admiration for poetry and philosophy in the modern world, but that such admiration does not constitute a space in which things are saved from destruction by time. The futility of public admiration, which daily is consumed in ever greater quantities, on the contrary, is such that monetary reward, one of the most futile things there is, can become more 'objective' and more real. (p204)

A PhD can be a place where a person can save ideas and ways of being in the world from destruction by time. There is no direct celebrity status or material gain from the act of writing and putting together a thesis, though the symbolic capital of cap and gown can be recognised as worth having. Through the project started by my PhD my contribution is to chart field claims and to ask about the spaces where knowledge claims can be uppermost. It is also to give recognition that the dust in the library is not waste in the form of dead knowledge but is alive through field scholarship.

6

Teachers, Postcoloniality and the PhD
Jennifer Lavia

Introduction

In this chapter, I seek to treat the issue of academic work as contested: as work which can be reconceptualised in terms of how context and culture influence experience rather than being taken for granted. In this undertaking, I contend that there is no single unifying truth that underpins academic study and, notwithstanding the demands of the Academy for an original contribution to knowledge, such endeavours are bound by the way in which they are experienced and represented. The lived experiences to which I refer are also shaped by the issues of positionality, culture, context and other such social phenomena. Consequently in this chapter, I acknowledge the seamless relationship between the personal and political and the ways in which social, historical and political configurations become manifest in the production of a PhD thesis.

A second undertaking of this chapter is to theorise the significance of writing from the perspective of a black Caribbean woman involved in innovative teacher education programmes conducted in the Caribbean by a British university. In this light, issues of race, class, gender and identity become central points of interrogating historical, colonial centre-periphery relations. Like McCarthy (1998), 'I have come to the growing recognition that my writing has been a form of postcolonial therapy, an exercise in opening up and pasting over contradictions of knowledge, place, context and belonging' (p1). Finding solace only in the exploration of oneself as heralded by Caribbean poet Derek Walcott (1986:18) and echoed by McCarthy, in the smallness of the state, 'this is the enigma of arrival of the postcolonial intellectual; [where] 'in the matter of her/his investigation of the subject of conflicted racial identity formation, the postcolonial soul can know no peace' (McCarthy, 1998:4). My PhD reflects a commitment to engendering a process of decolonisa-tion, one which embraces the complexity of identity, community and colonialism. In the midst of experiencing this thesis, I have been party to theory in practice.

Beginning in 1987, teachers in Trinidad, on their request, established a relationship with the University of Sheffield, with the aim of building capacity and developing a critical mass of educators in the twin island Republic of Trinidad and Tobago. I was fortunate to be part of early initiatives as well as subsequent development in the Caribbean region of the partnership between the University and teachers' unions and other academic institutions. Along with other teachers and academics, I was and continue to be involved in providing academic, adminis-trative and intellectual leadership to the programmes. The develop-ment of what is known today as the Sheffield Caribbean Programmes began from the bottom up, largely unrecognised by the Academy and having to create its own ways of being and doing as we went along.

I could present a chronological line of events and developments about the programmes but for me, personally, it was not quite that straight-forward because I have occupied multiple roles at one and the same time: student and lecturer and administrator and teacher in different combinations! It is against a background of these pioneering efforts and valued positions that I became involved in the University of Sheffield's first remote location PhD.

Positioning the study

My PhD research aimed to examine teacher development in Trinidad and Tobago in light of colonial and postcolonial education policy for-mation. In the thesis, I asserted that contemporary education policy has never transcended colonial attitudes regarding teachers and teach-ing. From the inception of the formal education system in 1851 in Trini-dad and Tobago, contested values over what constitutes professional identity have characterised colonial and postcolonial dispositions about teachers as an occupational group. Among these have been engagements over who is recognised to be a teacher, the autonomy and control of teachers, teachers' work and knowledge and teacher advocacy.

Further, I argued that the Education Act of 1966, which emerged within the context of the first wave of postcolonial education reforms, consolidated the central control of teachers by the state, constituted a single teaching service and integrated the teaching profession into the Public Service. Consequently, the Act, although representing structural and administrative changes to the governance of teachers in the era of political independence, endorsed and perpetuated the colonisation of teachers as a professional group.

My thesis paid attention to the state and education as well as the role of the intellectual in state development. Together, these theoretical positions allowed the thesis to adopt a critical, historical approach which was informed by the political and social contexts that have influenced conceptions of teacher professionalism in Trinidad and Tobago. Themes were generated based on analyses of the impact of global trends on national and historical developments. These themes were interrogated against a backdrop of colonial and postcolonial policy development, innovation in education and the role of education itself in state formation. Life histories and biographies of teachers served to provide insight into the policy process.

The study located the teacher at the centre of critical enquiry and demonstrated the relationship between the macro and micro arenas of policy (Fulcher, 1999), between structure and agency. In this sense the study adopted a postcolonial analysis that was decidedly aspirational by interrogating the hidden voices of teachers who were influential in advancing the anti-colonial, pro-nationalist movement in the 1940s, 50s and 60s.

The significance of the social and political history of Trinidad and Tobago is also elaborated and considered as a useful background to subsequent discussions in the study. The thesis of first prime minister of Trinidad and Tobago, Eric Williams, on the development of a nation state is instructive. Dr Williams was an ideologue, educator and politician of the liberal tradition. He emerged as leader of the nationalist movement from 1946, introduced party politics to this small state in 1956 and set about a decisive campaign of political education of the population. He states, 'four centuries of colonialism, from 1498 to 1897 had made Trinidad and Tobago a great workshop rather than a miniature state. A race had been freed, but a society had not yet been formed' (Williams, 1962:197).

To Williams, the legacy left by colonialism was a conglomeration of activities and events without identity and coherence.

Ever since the annihilation of the indigenous people, a process that began with Christopher Columbus on behalf of Spain in 1498, Trinidad and Tobago had been in a 'state of betweenity buffeted about from pillar to post, changing national flags and political allegiances' (Williams, 1962:123). Such allegiances gave rise to diverse entities from which a society was to be forged. Thus the history of Trinidad and Tobago is a history of conflict and contestation with the colonising might of the Spanish, French, British and Dutch being matched, at various times, with the resistance of the Amerindians, enslaved Africans and Indentured Servants from India, China and Portugal. Ultimately, the hodgepodge of influences and cultures had to be managed and governed. Williams' analysis was that education was the key to addressing the increasingly complex issues of diversity, and of forging a society.

Given the challenge thrown out by Williams, the PhD took on significance for the teacher who is concerned about the politics of the profession and the relationship between teaching and wider issues of social justice. In this light, my own involvement in study was more than as a disinterested party. I was intensely aware that my roles as teacher, trade union leader and political and social activist would influence decisions that I would make about the study.

The Ethnographic Self

When I finally submitted my thesis in April 2004 I, like American inspirational speaker, Iyanla Vanzant (2000) 'cried with an agenda'. I remember feeling that sense of relief that the proverbial baby was born, that the labour pains were intense but the baby was born! I sequestered myself almost in the same way as I had when I was in the final stages of writing up. I needed that place of silence to allow myself to let go now and begin to feel again a different set of emotions that I had so diligently repressed in order to just get through this process and finish the work.

I allowed myself to remember the times when I should have picked up my son from school but forgot because I was at a union meeting and the time and intensity of the meeting simply took precedence. I remembered the various family occasions, especially the vacation trips to Tobago which I missed because I had to get the chapter done. I remembered the late nights and very early mornings when I fell asleep at the computer only to realise that my son was asleep on my lap because he had insisted on staying up with me to keep me company. I wept silently. I wept and allowed myself to remember how I had to negotiate time with my family and the various ways I tried to over compensate for my absence. I especially wept when I remembered how that absence was used as an excuse for marital indiscretions just a few months before I had to submit the thesis; yet I cried about how I was able to turn such disappointment and hurt into life lessons and carry on with determination to successful completion. It was an empowering moment when I allowed myself to 'cry with an agenda', with a hopefulness!

When I first decided to do a PhD I was completing the last of six years with the teachers' union. Indeed, it was quite by chance that I decided to do it since I had hoped and longed for a much needed rest from the hectic pace of union activities. I had hoped that after my term of office had ended, I would be able to make up for the days and nights and weekends away from the family and in particular my young son that were otherwise spent attending to teachers' matters. However, the opportunity to do a PhD with the University of Sheffield was presented when as an extension of a long and successful relationship with teachers in Trinidad and Tobago, the University agreed to offer the first remote location PhD in Trinidad. What was important was that an opportunity was presented to do doctoral studies part time at home, at a time when I was already overcome by guilt about keeping horrendously long hours at work and running my self ragged in my attempts to make up and be a good mother, wife, daughter, sister, aunt and friend.

In the thesis I recognised the usefulness of constructing and appending a time-line which I titled *The Ethnographic Self and the Policy Process,* which I used as an analytical tool to explore the intersection of history and biography. I found out as I dwelled on this aspect of the research that it was possible to gain insights into the policy process while using critical incidents within my own narrative. By explicating these critical incidents I related educational policy to the lived experience of the 'subject'. This discourse sought to add 'participant structured conversations' and accounts as part of 'the research repertoire' (Casey, 1995:239).

I also chose to initiate the ethnographic case with my own beginnings. The 1950s and 1960s provided critical incidents of a personal and political nature. I was born at a time when new constitutional arrangements sanctioned elections being held to the first fully elected Legislature in Trinidad and Tobago. By September of that year, Eric Williams and the People's National Movement had won a landslide victory at the polls. Dr Williams was elected Chief Minister of Trinidad and Tobago at the first sitting of the Parliament. There is consensus, in common sense terms and by academics and researchers alike (Brereton, 1986; Ryan, 1971; Campbell, 1987; 1997), that these events marked the introduction of party politics in the territory. It also legitimated the movement towards nationalism and a new dispensation in the decolonisation process.

My father and his four brothers had been part of the fortunate group of young black colonials who had the opportunity to attend the first state run college of the colonial government, while his seven sisters all attended the preferred institution for the education of elite Anglican girls. My mother, on the other hand, attended a Catholic girls' schools run by St. Joseph of Cluny nuns, which catered for the education of non-white Catholic girls. The common elements are evident: progress through education as a key ingredient in the social mobility of the black middle class (Brereton, 1985); the distinctly urban world view; and faith as a source of survival.

I entered primary school in 1960, the year of the historic signing of the Concordat, at the dawn of political independence and in the midst of the restructuring of the systems of education and schooling. I attended the primary school at which my mother and aunt taught. The presence of senior students characterised its status as an Intermediate school offering a curriculum from the Infant classes (4-5 years of age) to Form Five (16-17 years). Such Catholic Intermediate schools were permitted, designed to offer a form of vocational education for girls while maintaining a few core classical subjects. Ironically, Pure Sciences and Mathematics were not considered necessary or desirable for the girls at the school.

My cohort was the last group to be recruited as part of the Intermediate school system, which was eventually phased out in the late 1960s. To accommodate the transition from Intermediate status to full secondary school status, the school put up a new building. I vividly remember having to remove the desks and chairs from the old building and carry them to the new one. The 'new school' brought with it changes to the curriculum. English and Mathematics became compulsory and the sciences were introduced over a period of time.

From my earliest memory, I was surrounded by family discussions about nationalism, about the role of the public service (my father was a senior public officer) and the role of the teacher (my maternal lineage). Public political meetings of the newly formed People's National Movement (PNM) and its political education programme were transferred to the living room and around the dining table of my home. From the social gatherings of friends and those among the family, the topic of debate was always 'teacher talk' (Middleton and May, 1997) or problems of the newly independent state.

As a senior public servant my father frequently vented his frustration at having to match the political agenda of the state with the realities of his practice as a public officer. In the case of my mother, the tensions of being a teacher with a denominational board were effectively discharged in informal settings that were safe and free from reprisal (usually in the staff room over lunch!). The challenge of teacher education was clearly articulated by a maternal aunt who, as a teacher educator and later school supervisor, frequently got into conflict with those who sought to restrict her creativity on grounds of either gender or policy.

My own sense of social justice was also strenthened by the Black Power movement in the 1970s. This movement had taken root in significant ways in the Caribbean and the cry for equality and equity of the black population in Trinidad and Tobago resonated in significant ways amongst a large section of the population who rejected the perpetuation of legacies of colonialism. The sentiments were varied yet unified in the desire to live a better life that was determined on our terms. For those of us who were still at secondary school, the very successful and high profile students' movement resulted in most schools establishing student councils and forums for wider social and political debates. I became vice-president of my school's student council.

From those early beginnings something gnawed away deep within me, beckoning me to resist injustice and exclusion. At a strategic level, this personal narrative elucidates the influence upon my own worldview of being and knowing. At a practical level, I learnt from sitting at the feet of my parents and grandparents and listening to the frequent political and educational discussions among friends and family in informal settings. I learnt through modeling, my own conception of a teacher being sensitively crafted by the examples of my predecessors. It was evident (though not straightforward) that my research would have been influenced by a sense of conversation that formed a central feature of the family setting and political encounters. The 'dialogic principle' (Freire, 1985) was alive!

There was no issue about world events or local issues upon which the elders did not have a view. The discussions were wide ranging and child and adult alike took part. These memories allowed me to draw on the strength of my ancestors and my own experiences as an undergraduate, teacher and social activist to elaborate broad policy constructs that had helped to shape and frame the lived experiences that I was intending to represent in my thesis. These early biographical reflections led me into wanting to explore further the relationship between teachers and a politics of change.

The location of teachers in social change

The notion of the role of the intellectual in state formation is apposite to any discussion about social change in Trinidad and Tobago since 'the teachers were in fact the leaders of the Independence movement' (Bajunid, 2000:178) and the new nation state required a consolidated intelligentsia to expedite its platform of public education. According to Gramsci, 'there is no human activity from which every form of intellectual participation can be excluded' and everyone, outside his or her particular professional activity...

carries on some form of intellectual activity, participates in a particular conception of the world, has a conscious line of moral conduct, and therefore contributes to sustain a conception of the world or to modify it, that is, to bring into being new modes of thought. (Gramsci, 1971:9)

In this sense, the nationalist forces in the 1940s, 1950s and 1960s were progressive and essential to political transformation. Nonetheless, my study considered the ways in which 'power, ideology and control are implicated in the educational arrangements', and the pivotal role played by the social-historical location of teachers as 'a crucial sector of the agents of cultural and social reproduction' and transformation (Grace, 1978:1). I recognised and grew restless with the understanding that, as Grace articulates:

The need to control the teachers of the people by keeping before them anticipations of respectability and social honour epitomised in the concept of a profession, was a strategy which was to have a long history. (Grace, 1978: 15)

This sentiment is echoed by Ball (2001:10). In asserting the centrality of teachers as 'public intellectuals', he opines that, in the UK at least, the effect of education policy, particularly in the 1980s, has caused 'the taming of the teacher.' He observes how 'control and discipline' of the teacher is manifested in the ways policy currently seeks 'to capture, specify and delineate 'the teacher'. However, McCulloch *et al* (2000) argue that there is a tendency toward idealising professionalism to the extent that the notion (myth) of curriculum and occupational autonomy in the 1960s and 1970s enjoyed primacy. While Ball and McCulloch were both writing about the UK, and particularly England and Wales, their general comments can be extrapolated to similar conditions in other national contexts.

Consideration of teachers 'as a strategic occupation group' (Grace, 1978:3) in the postcolonial state requires critical engagement about contested values and interests. What I sought to employ was a practice of 'critical professionalism' to interrogate intellectual and moral leadership; the generation of cultural values through the lives and careers of teachers; and a consideration of teacher professionalism as symbolic of political and professional control on the one hand and, on the other, a necessary element of social change characterised by political struggle.

In the thesis I presented my empirical chapters in two parts, each bearing relation to the dialectical relationship between teachers and society. I explored ways in which teacher identities were crafted through strictures of national policy on teacher education, recruitment and retention and classification. According to Bernstein (1971), 'how a society selects, classifies, distributes, transmits and evaluates the educational knowledge it considers to be public, reflects both the distribution of power and the principles of social control' (p 47).

In the age of political independence, teachers were 'a strategic occupational group' (Grace, 1978:3). Colonialism, in many ways had consistently whittled away at the dignity of the teachers while at the same time, the lack of a developed centralised system allowed for the educational enterprise to be effected mainly within the school. Even when punitive action was taken against teachers who dared to challenge the *status quo*, they were often able to convert their 'punishment' into a worthwhile experience of community involvement.

In Bernstein's terms, then, society does impact on the experience of the individual and group through the media of 'curriculum, pedagogy and evaluation' (Grace, 1978:47). Consequently, articulations about teacher professionalism are to be examined in light of the ways in which society mediates, negotiates and makes public, images and understandings of teachers and teaching. These public articulations are also found in policies. In Trinidad and Tobago, the 1966 Education Act symbolised a range of meanings and interpretations about teacher professionalism that were not necessarily dissimilar to those of the colonial era. Guidelines about who could be a teacher, what would constitute teachers' knowledge, and where teachers were to learn, under what conditions teachers were to work and what they were supposed to do, are enshrined not only in the text but also in the structure of experiences.

However, I also examined how teachers influenced society and how through their agency they constructed their own images of their professional identity. I was particularly interested in locating the points of interruption of the legacies of colonialism where teachers demonstrated agency, so exemplifying that teaching is a political act and elaborating 'the complexity of the school teacher as an active agent making his or her own history' (Goodson, 2000:15).

It seemed important to me that the thesis confront the notion of sub-jugation as the dominant perception of the teacher and illustrate the ways in which teacher identities have been shaped through teachers' involvement in broader undertakings than those of the classroom. To add a caveat, however, it is not to be misconstrued that such undertak-ings occur in isolation from each other. Rather, the interplay between teachers and society is a dialectical process of negotiation and media-tion, with each influencing the other and the outcomes of that process being represented as products of tension-filled interactions.

My PhD, therefore, represented my understanding of such interactions through discourses of teachers' perceptions of their profession and the factors that influenced them to become teachers: firstly through the concept of commitment; secondly, through a construction of the social history of teacher unionism and examining the ways in which sectarian organisations were used to impose a conservative notion of teacher professionalism in opposition to what was perceived as the radicalism of teacher unionism. I also considered issues of occupational segrega-tion and attempts at unification. Thirdly, I looked at how teachers chose to create new forms of organisation and thus create a new culture for teachers.

Teachers creating a new culture

In the PhD I found myself moving back and forth in my reflections about my roles as pedagogue and activist. I came to realise that despite the multiplicity of social roles I had come to an understanding that my practice was all-encompassing – fraught with political considerations and contradictions. Whether as a trade union officer or classroom teacher, creative strategies and innovation were essential dispositions for survival, empowerment, recognition and the creation of new solu-tions.

During my years as a secondary school teacher I became involved in organising intra and extra mural activities and in involving parents and the wider community in the school's events. Through my combined teaching disciplines of physical education and inclusive education, and active pursuit of creating new and varied images of my practice, I thought I would expose my students, most of whom were rejected and ejected from the mainstream subject areas, to a wide range of cultural experiences. Accordingly, I began working on developing alternative curricula, through productive partnerships with teachers, parents and students.

Essentially, my philosophy was one of inclusion, involvement and creativity, but it was not to be restricted to the classroom. Its realisation required the participation of teachers and the school, and of parents and the wider community, as it aimed to extend the learning environment beyond the classroom and traditional academic subjects. Involvement would also mean parents, teachers and students working collaboratively on developing the curriculum. It was in the search for evidence that I came to realise that the notion of teachers developing a broad-based pedagogy – a pedagogy for economic and cultural development – was not a new feature of life for teachers in Trinidad and Tobago. Although not well articulated, such a tradition had been established by a group of progressive teachers who formed the Teachers', Economic and Cultural Association Limited (TECA) in the 1940s and who were able to sustain the organisation well into the period of political independence. Through the PhD I was able to examine the significance of TECA and became inspired and buoyed by their efforts. Mirza (2009) emphasises the importance of being inspired by others and learning from them.

A critical case study of TECA provided insights into how and why teachers gave expression to their struggle against the colonial condition and the legacies and traditions that have emerged from it. TECA emerged within the context of disaffection with the colonial condition. In recounting the conditions that gave rise to this particular organisation Oxaal (1982) states:

> A negative image of the colonial past would play a major role in legitimising the demand for independence, but it was of course, only part of the story. The post-slavery century in Trinidad produced local legends, traditions and social relationships which not only conditioned the form the nationalist movement itself would take, but provided an indisputable residue of collective memories and meanings without which a nationalist movement in this implausible island could not have emerged at all. (p33)

TECA undertook a movement of conscious action and a pedagogy of hope, freedom and national development that placed the teacher at the centre. Disenchantment among teachers about the role and function of the teachers' union and the attempts by colonial education policy to undermine their professional practice was not new to the teachers of the 1930s, 1940s and 1950s. What was new, however, was the extent to which they showed their discontent by creating new forms of expression. These new forms of expression would lay the foundation for future political, economic and cultural traditions, not only among teachers but also among the wider society. Therefore a study of the role and significance of the TECA to national development and the creation of alternative images of teachers' identities became important for inclusion in the thesis.

TECA also represented a level of teacher activism through which a new culture for teachers was forged. According to the organisation's First Deputy Director General W J Alexander (in Oxaal, 1982):

> We were the victims, par excellence, of colonialism. We wanted to organise the teachers effectively, to improve their lot economically while at the same time making a cultural contribution to the community. (p3)

These sentiments are echoed by TECA's Director General, D W Rogers and its statistician Donald Pierre who formulated the following impressions about the organisation:

> At the time of its foundation a number of younger teachers, who considered themselves to be more socially conscious than the average, came to the conclusion that the official teachers' union was moribund. A common complaint was that it had little support from the teachers and failed to give voice in a militant way to their grievances against the dual system of education. The system of dual control of church and state had produced some felt, flagrant examples of the victimisation of teachers who failed to toe the mark according to the wishes of the authorities and, of course, there was always the question of attempting to raise the salaries and improve working conditions, In addition, there were frequent conflicts between teachers and the denominational boards arising from diverging religious outlooks among teachers and administrators. White expatriate instructors and administrators, particularly in the Roman Catholic Schools, were often alleged to discriminate against teachers and students on the basis of color. (Oxaal, 1982:3)

It was not surprising, therefore, that TECA adopted as its motto: The Progress of the Teacher, the Uplift of the People. TECA had been spearheaded by a progressive cohort of teachers who had become disgruntled with the pedantic operations of the teachers' union and who found the reactive approach limiting to the professionalism of teachers. It is this limitation that prodded these teachers to form TECA as a broad based organisation of teachers that emphasised the centrality of teachers and which located teachers at the centre of a political movement.

During TECA's existence, a new culture was created among teachers. It was a cultural renaissance, it was reformation in education, and it was a critical period for rethinking and recontextualising the role of teachers. In order to ready itself for political independence, the state had to address and redress the ills that were affecting the teaching service and, as a consequence, the entire education system. In turn, teachers had taken leadership of not merely attending to their needs but also linking their improvement to that of the uplift of society. The relationship between pedagogy and the struggle for social justice was consolidated as interrelated aspects of what teachers did.

The significance of TECA is three-fold. In the first instance, TECA represented defiance by teachers to be openly critical of colonial education. Secondly, it provided and promoted economic self-reliance for teachers as a pillar of teachers' emancipation through the purchase of shares. Thirdly, TECA laid the foundation for new forms of political organisation and action. In particular, it emphasised the need for action based on research and evidence. TECA's impact on education and national development can be recorded as clearly pivotal. From inception, the organisation had clear aims about its political direction and intent. However, it was not until the post World War Two phase that the organisation became as public and political as it was. The global influence of the cooperative movement, socialism, the women's movement and the decline of Britain as a colonial power provided the fillip the organisation needed in order to effect its agenda.

The Teachers' Movement

My interest in how teachers' organisations have impacted on the construction of teachers' identity was not fleeting. My second entry into teaching in the late 1970s was at the secondary school level – the first being at primary level in the early 1970s – and almost from the inception of my new appointment I voluntarily joined the new movement of teachers. This movement was challenging the *status quo* which provided for three unions to represent teachers' interests. In fact, the 1966 Education Act enshrined in law the names of the three unions and debarred any other union from being formed and being recognised by the government as a bargaining body for teachers. The Committee for the Unification of Teachers (COMFUT) emerged as the forerunner to the Trinidad and Tobago Unified Teachers' Association (TTUTA), which made a successful bid to challenge the constitutionality of the existing legislative provision in 1981. According to the official documents of the TTUTA:

> Teachers had been struggling for many years to form a truly democratic, representative body. They had found oppressive, the absence of proper representation by the three existing teacher organisations recognised by the Education Act No. 1 of 1966. In March 1979, they heeded a call for unity by Frank B. Seepersad and the members of the steering committee for the Unification of Teachers (COMFUT). More than ten thousand signatures were attached to the petition outlining the clear intention of the teachers. The government outdid its colonial political mentors by doing everything in its power to frustrate the teachers' movement. (TTUTA, 1991:20)

By 1979, a constitution for TTUTA was framed outlining a democratic framework of one man one vote and the division of the organisation into semi-autonomous districts, thus assuring members that nepotism and having leaders for life favoured in the old teachers unions would not be permitted in the new organisation. The Constitution also affirmed the organisation's aim as 'the promotion of the cause of education and the professional, economic, spiritual and social well-being of its members' (TTUTA, 1981). The nation wide campaign was filtered through mass public meetings, marches to Parliament and other government buildings, letters and petitions, insider lobbying and a range of solidarity activities including 'marches, withdrawal of enthusiasm, wearing red [clothing]' (TTUTA, 1991:21).

After serving as a staff representative I moved onto zonal and district representation. Enough persuasion from several quarters induced me to seek elected national office. I won the post of first vice president and undertook a portfolio which included teacher education, professional development and education policy. I undertook the task with enthusiasm albeit with no experience at national office. But I was armed with a notion that teachers had power and that they should be supported to live and work with the conscious realisation of that power. As the lone female on the team and at the Central Executive (comprising 19 persons), I was abundantly aware that I would be under the scrutiny of my peers as well as the wider membership. The resistance to issues raised with regard to the role of women in the union did not surprise me. It did reflect, however, that I would have to employ creative strategies for the portfolio were I to be granted more than lip service.

Feminist consciousness

I share with Miriam David (2003) a long ambiguous relationship with feminist ideologies where 'my own intellectual and professional journey has been rather circuitous'. Although I was involved in feminist activities and the women's movements of the 1970s and 1980s, as a young woman I took this involvement for granted and never constructed it consciously as a feminist project; its development was, rather, organic (Mirza, 2009). During the 1970s whilst in Canada doing my undergraduate studies, I recognised that I was struggling to find my voice within the women's movement and the wider revolutionary cause of class struggle because I was black and middle class. There were hints of other identity issues that emerged to resonate with what it felt like being a black Caribbean woman, but the political movement then gave priority to the class struggle so issues of race and gender (though acknowledged) took second place. I found myself preoccupied with vying for recognition of women within these progressive movements and being ostracised at times by the largely hierarchical male dominated leadership.

Yet, as I would come to realise later on in life (culminating in doing the PhD) my early and continued involvement with the politics and activities of feminism had profoundly and positively influenced my developing cultural and political confidence. The PhD therefore became the apotheosis of cultural and psychological deconstruction through narrative critique where 'searching for meaning among various political and social movements was a significant process within the broader movement for social change' (David, 2003:30).

Doing the PhD was therefore unsettling. It was filled with interrogations of taken for granted assumptions and the compelling requirement to treat the familiar as strange. I was drawn to reflect on Frantz Fanon's (1967) notion of ways in which the experience of colonialism has shaped both the coloniser and the colonised and how the colonised bears witness internally 'to the resultant imbalance in relations of power' (Asher, 2009:3). From the outset I wrestled with tensions over voice, representation and identity, as I was well aware that I wanted the thesis to make a positive contribution to understanding the lives of women teachers. I recognised this as important because, although the study did not profess to provide feminist analysis, the data generated indicated that the conditions and location of women teachers during the period under consideration required detailed attention.

According to Apple (in Casey, 1993:xiii), 'for women teachers, the personal has always been the political, in part because of the history of the ways teachers have been regulated in both their public and private lives'. In the context of Trinidad and Tobago, the history is one of resistance to discrimination over equality of salaries, opportunities to promotion and higher education.

I recognised that interpretations of how women experienced teaching have been largely neglected and unrecorded. Their understanding of their condition has never been regarded as important or a significant source for policy analysis. Yet in the stories collected from the women teachers interviewed, each one had a lucid and involved role to play in educational development as well as national development. Interestingly, they were generally reluctant to talk about such involvement because they felt that it just came naturally.

In unearthing such history, I found that one of the most outstanding features of early political movement of teachers (particularly through TECA) was the way in which women teachers were actively involved in large numbers. These women were not just passive members; they were part of the group of activists who took the passion of teacher education and mass mobilising as an educational and pedagogical exercise.

The case of unequal salaries and discrimination was also linked to the education of girls. By 1948, there was a growing movement for the greater participation of women and girls in the education system. The concern for the education for young girls and women has had the consequence of women teachers developing a language of resistance. What might appear to be subservience was in fact a form of activism that allowed them to gain access to places and information that was needed for the movement. What the women teachers also brought to the movement was 'the care these women gave to their students; the outrage they feel towards injustice and the way they dare to sue the limited power that they have' (Casey, 1993:166). In other words, they created opportunities and political possibilities.

Conclusion: Decolonisation and the self

The process of unearthing and representing the dynamics (shifts and images) of key policy moments can also be extended to an investigation into the ways in which evidence is generated. It brings with it 'a form of reflective, acquired self-knowledge' (Carr, 1995:115) which Habermas (1972) refers to as 'emancipatory knowledge'; to this notion can be added the Freirean concept of 'conscientisation'. Conscientisation is a process of critical reflection that embraces questions about the ways in which people represent images and connections about themselves and society (Freire, 1985). The notion of emancipation, therefore, is to be considered in light of the dialectic between 'determinism and freedom' (Freire, 1985:68). It also embraces the 'personhood' of the researcher and challenges the researcher 'to see beyond the contingencies that have made us in a quest for freedom' (Kendall and Wickham, 1999:34). My own history, work, culture and values (Freire, 1985) shaped by the experience of being and living in the field were to be recognised in the critical authorship of the study.

The PhD was a process of decolonisation which began a project that acknowledged the synergies between the personal, the political, the intellectual and the academic. Through ownership of the work, I engaged with issues of colonialism, identity and inner vision and gained cultural and academic confidence. Decolonisation was an engagement of praxis 'that drew on personal experiences and biographies or autobiographies as ways to capture the essence of family life and its relation to social and economic transformations ad social structures' (David, 2003:124).

Theoretically and methodologically celebrating the elders in the PhD meant recognising survival, resistance and resilience. It meant remembering 'not just what colonisation was about' but the ways in which each story reflected the experience of change, innovation and development. It represented ways of connecting with the elders in a respectful manner, honouring their dignity and facilitating a humanising process. It meant negotiating a space and seeking their tacit and formal permission to represent their voice. The interview group represented a wide range of experiences and influences. Their voices represented many years of experience within the system and provided invaluable data about the experience of classroom teachers as well as administrators, the relationship between teachers and society, as well as the teacher's role in the community (Lavia, 2004, 2006; Smith, 1999).

It is evident that personal and textual development and transformation occur simultaneously in the process of the practice itself (Coffey, 1999). Further, 'the ways we think of research and write are always outcomes of the possibilities and constraints of our historical, material, cultural, political, institutional and biographical, circumstances' (Middleton, 1995: 3). Goodson and Sikes (2001:36) concur with Middleton's position, articulating that 'the way in which researchers go about analysing evidence is in itself influenced by the epistemological and philosophical position they take'. To return to Coffey's argument, social inquiry is thus 'one of the central ways in which the emotionality and passion of the fieldwork are enacted' (Coffey, 1999:137).

Textual and field experiences were central in providing the language for me to articulate how I was being transformed academically, spiritually and intellectually through the doctoral process. The experiences led me into 'ethnographic excursions, seeking out new understandings in new places in the realm of imagination and in the quiet agonism of postcolonial self-exploration and self understanding' (McCarthy, 1998:4). These encounters were life lessons. They are underscored by Mirza's sobering advice: 'we have to look for patterns in the quilt, patterns which go against the grain of formal social expectations. We have to see round corners' and look at things differently, chart the hidden histories (Mirza, 2009:153).

7

Love in the cupboard: a conversation about success and sadness when race, gender and class collide in the making of an academic career

Heidi Safia Mirza and Kate Hoskins

Introduction: Heidi Safia Mirza

This autobiographical conversation with Kate Hoskins tells of my journey into academe and how I came to write my PhD. It is a personal insider's account of the complex and multiple ways in which the dynamics of class, gender and race shaped my career path. The interview describes the success and sadness I have experienced as a postcolonial woman of colour living and working in the academy in 21st century Britain.

My academic life has spanned three decades. My first book, *Young, Female and Black* (1992) was my PhD thesis. It was a small scale ethnography of Caribbean young women in a London school. I grew up in Trinidad in the Caribbean but went to school in London in 1970s. My PhD was about my own life and experiences. I wanted to research and write about second generation Caribbean young women in British schools and the interplay between career choices, aspirations and educational structures. My PhD was, in effect, both an academic and an autobiographical journey. On reflection, exploring the exclusionary practices of gendered racism which I saw around me was a cathartic process. In this sense academic writing based on autobiography can be like a mask. You can use academic theory and academic conventions to articulate, in a very objective and distanced way, something that you've experienced yourself, but you are not really naming it or implicating yourself emotionally in it.

As I speak to Kate and then read my words in print I find my story revealing, embarrassing, discontinuous and cleansing all at once. Who am I? What do I want the world to know about me? Who is my audience and how honest can I be? I find it hard to read my own talk. Would I have said something different about my academic journey and the consequence of the PhD a year ago, or a year from now? These questions demonstrate the destabilising effects of autobiographical narrative and the methodological boundaries of the interview process which highlight the contingent specificity of data captured in talk. Autobiography is a reflexive method that empowers the teller's interpretation of the past (Cosslett *et al*, 2000). It is a powerful tool and individual stories illuminate the collective effects of discursive processes that construct our social and political worlds. Black Feminism complements this methodology as it seeks to make sense of the black female woman's symbolic and narrative struggle over the defining materiality of her othered experience (Mirza, 2009). Thus a reflexive and experiential positioning of the self in theory is fundamental to a Black Feminist position. My narrative is grounded in this theoretical standpoint.

The interview reveals the multiple and complex ways structures of power reproduce social divisions in the happenchance of my black/ethnicised woman's life chances and educational opportunities. By mapping the embodied intersectionality of my experience, the interview about my journey up to and beyond the PhD reveals social processes and systematic institutionalised discriminatory practices in the context of my classed, raced and gendered human agency. How do class, race, and gender distinctions structure my subjectivity as an othered woman of colour in our overwhelmingly dominant white places of teaching and learning? This question addresses the issue of black/ethnicised female identity and subjectivity and the way difference is systematically organised through social relations in our political and economic structures, polices and practices (Mirza, 2009).

It is up to the reader to interpret and unpack the interrelationship between dominant structures and systems of class, race and gender in my evolving story of seeming academic success. It is a privilege to share with you such a space of conscious reflection.

Introduction: Kate Hoskins

This interview with Heidi Mirza was conducted as part of my doctoral research, which involved interviewing twenty female professors on their perceptions and constructions of their career success and how these are influenced by the women's social class, gender and race.

The irony of this interview about Heidi's academic journey into the academy and doing her PhD is that it in turn is nourishing my PhD. Talking to Heidi gave me insights into the influence of her class background, gender and ethnicity in shaping the way she describes her success; her story is my PhD data. The cycle of mentor/mentee plays out between us – each giving in and giving back to the PhD process.

Reading this interview between Heidi and myself allows me to reflect on the methodological limitations of interviewing and the limitations of using narratives for my PhD. As a researcher the question for me throughout the research process is how to present my respondents' stories as 'accurate representations' (Hammersley, 2003:123). I was particularly struck by Heidi's remark ,'you caught me on a bad day, my first day back', and I wondered in what ways our conversation would have been different on another day. How will I account for the historical specificity of Heidi's story, as it evolved and was produced in our interview? Is it possible, given the complexity of social realities, to capture in an interview anything more than a snapshot in time? Heidi's story is historically grounded and the views she has expressed are fluid and subject to change as she constructs and reconstructs her social reality. Acknowledging this, I recognise that my presentation of her life story will be partial and incomplete; an insight into a story in progress rather than a final or conclusive account.

Doing interviews also raises important questions about the use of other people's stories for research and the way they are represented in the text. For example how should I take decisions about what data to include and omit from Heidi's narrative in my PhD thesis and on what basis should these choices be made? Representation is a complex and subjective task because the researcher has the power potentially to silence the voices of those for whom they speak. As Kirsch argues, 'representation can become misrepresentation, the reinforcement of unjust power structures and institutional hierarchies' (1999:46). Ambiguity in representing a person's story is partly attributable to the complexity of the historically specific intersections of class, gender and race in an individual's identity. Interview accounts are open to multiple interpretations and it is possible to offer an account of a life story that the respondent might not accept as an entirely faithful portrayal. Thus, in approaching the issue of representation it is important for me, the re-searcher, to be reflexive in accounting for my presence in the research process as it is a central factor in the end product created.

It was a privilege for me to share Heidi's space of conscious reflections. For the moment, I leave it up to readers to construct their own inter-pretations of the representations in Heidi's account.

Heidi Safia Mirza in conversation with Kate Hoskins

KH   Thank you for agreeing to be interviewed. First question, can you tell me a little bit about your family background?

HM   My mum is Austrian, and she met my father, who is Indo-Caribbean, here in London in the fifties. They had myself and my brother, and went to live in Trinidad when I was four years old. So it's kind of a modern day, mixed race, multicultural story. I always wanted to write a book about their relationship. I wanted to call it 'Love in the Cupboard', because when my dad married my mum he was so afraid of his father, that he hid her in a cupboard! His father was a very strict minister in the Presbyterian church in Trinidad and came to visit my dad in England when he was a student. But my dad had already secretly married my mum and because she was white, and not from back home, he hid her in the cupboard during his father's visit. They sat down on the bed, in his bedsit, and had tea while my mum was tucked up in the cupboard in the same room! So the book 'Love in the Cupboard' would be about the taboos there were on those kind of relationships back then. This was the 1950s, it was that whole period of no dogs, no Irish, no blacks wanted here. So it was a very difficult time on all sides, and a very brave move for both of them.

KH   What about their position in relation to class?

HM   I would say that it's very hard to unpack notions of social class as we understand it in the British context, because they both came from very different cultures where understandings of class are very different. My father came from Trinidad, from very humble origins. I went back and visited where he grew up. It was a small wooden house in the middle of the Island. It was very remote, reached through mountains and jungle. My grandfather, as I said, was a minister in the church there, and this would have been in the 1920s through to the '40s.

     I suppose what really defined social class in those contexts was whether you'd had an education or not. My grandfather was one of the first local people to actually achieve the status of a minister at the turn of the century, and that was quite a high position. The Canadian missionaries were operating at the time throughout the West Indian islands, and so my father had access to some education, and worked his way through what was called the monitorial system there. So he was able to come to England in the 1950s, as a reasonably well educated person, to come here and study, and finish his studies in accounting. He was, I suppose, in a sense, relatively privileged. Although if you were comparing it to a British notion of social class... no, I don't know if it's comparable really.

     In the 1950s and 60s there was a whole post-colonial shift with the emergence of the new independent nation states in Africa and the Caribbean. These countries were beginning to find their own self-determination in becoming free – no longer British colonies. So there was a sense in which anybody who was educated would become part of the next elite, or would be the new managerial classes. So there was a sense in which my father was being...not groomed, but would be part of that generation. That's why we went back, that and the fact he could not get a good job in England because of racism. Trinidad just got its independence and my father got a job in an oil company. Trinidad has a lot of oil! So he had a relatively good position by the time he returned from England ... so he came from very humble origins, but then returned to work in one of the nationalised industries as a professional.

KH   Right.

HM   So, yes, I would say that we would be middle class by the time we were growing up.

KH   Yes.

HM   But my father still retained all those things, like he wouldn't buy himself new socks, or he wouldn't ... you know, he held on to a lot of things to do with the poverty of his upbringing. And my mother was from very humble origins too, and I like to tease her, that she was born in a barn. She was! In Austria! It was a very rural part of Austria, and she always said that it was her destiny to leave. An opportunity arose when a family was passing through the small village where she lived, which was a coal mining village. In fact her father used to work in the coal mines. He had a pit pony. She's shown me pictures where he didn't have a thumb, because the horse had bitten it off. But anyway, that's how I learnt about their backgrounds. Her mother was just such a wonderful hard working, loving woman. She was tiny, round and about four foot tall, and wore a headscarf. A rich family was passing through their village, and needed an *au pair* to look after their kids as they were travelling through Europe. My mum was nineteen, I think, at the time. So she got to visit all the countries of Europe and ended up in England, looking after the children. And then she met my dad, who was in the international students' association, at the Queen's Coronation Ball, because the person she was *au paring* for had a free ticket, and they couldn't go, and they said, would you like to go? And then she met my dad!

So they were both from very humble origins, but I would say that they've done quite well, I suppose. My mum's a beautician now and she runs her own business in Trinidad, and she does self help and healing and alternative therapies. There was no expectation though that I should go to university, and that's because it was a very gendered time and the expectation was that I would get married to, probably, somebody of that emerging elite. At the time in the sixties and the seventies that would be my fate. To marry a lawyer, a doctor, an accountant, a dentist, oh, God forbid! Anyway ... that would have been my fate.

KH   When you were much younger, growing up, can you recall having any ambitions for possible future careers for yourself?

HM   I had none whatsoever. I used to have crazy girl fantasies that I would be rich and famous and marry David Cassidy or Germane Jackson...we had a lot of American TV in Trinidad! Later, thank god it was Che Guevara! But no, I had no real expectations of having a career. It wasn't something that I was brought up to do. We didn't have many books in the house – that is another thing that I always remember. We had *Readers' Digest* and the *Encyclopaedia Britannica*, but my parents weren't great readers and there wasn't that kind of academic atmosphere at all. No.

KH So going now to your current job, can you tell me a little bit about why you enjoy your current work?

HM That's assuming I do enjoy it!

KH That is assuming that you do enjoy it. And so the next question is, can you tell me why you don't enjoy it?

HM I have to be really honest and say that I struggle every day with this job. I am Professor of Equalities Studies in Education here at the Institute. I'm passionate about my subject and deeply committed to women's rights and the struggle against racism, but University is not a natural place for me, and I don't know how I've ended up here. It was never a conscious decision of mine. What happened is...and I was just saying this to my partner the other day, the British educational system gave me opportunities, which are not available now, through the grant system in the '70s.

I was schooled up until the age of 16 in the Caribbean, in Trinidad. I went to an all girls' school there, which was quite high achieving, but in a gendered way. High achieving girls did not necessarily mean career girls; it meant good wives for good husbands. In fact the school was started up by my grandmother about thirty years before I had gone there. As I was saying, there was a tradition of education in the family. In fact, my aunts were all teachers, but there wasn't a sense that girls had careers. Teaching children was not a career as such.

When we came back here to England I went to a local school in Brixton, and oh, the racism was incredible. I had a very strong Caribbean accent, which I've learnt to change over the years in order to transcend the stereotyped box that you were put into, which is how you were racialised. That was in the early '70s and I was about 16. I was determined to show the teachers and the girls in the school that I was as good as them, if not better. And that's what really drove me to do quite well in my O and A levels, and then getting a place at university that was then funded through the grant system. I think if it hadn't been a free place at university I would have never gone.

KH So you think it was a happy chance of the circumstance, rather than any sense of a planned progression.

HM Yes, there was no plan of progression. It was just like, 'what are you going to do when you finish your A levels, as you've done quite well? Well, you go to university, because that is available'. In the 70s there was this whole expansion of higher education. There was the grant system, and so I had my accommodation and fees and everything, which you wouldn't get today. If I was growing up today I would not have that chance.

KH   So do you think you were lucky?

HM   It isn't luck because that was an opportunity that was open for everybody. You know, higher education was being opened out for the working classes, and for girls as well, and it was seen as a natural progression, even by the school. I wasn't encouraged by my school to go to university, I have to say. There were favourites in the school, and I wasn't one of them. I was seen as precocious as I wanted to go to Oxford and Cambridge, because that's what I thought a university was! They told me I'd never make it, and I should try to do other things, like typing. And then one day I remember going upstairs to the careers room. It was a very sad room with old prospectuses in, and I saw one for the University of East Anglia, and I thought: that looks really nice. I loved the way the buildings looked like blocks, and the fields, and I'd never been to the English countryside, and I just thought – oh, that looks really good. They were offering something called Development Studies, which was Third World development, and I was all very gung ho about colonialism and, you know, very politically minded, and I just thought – that looks like a good place. Then I put it down on my application form, and off I went. That kind of sealed my fate. So I wouldn't call it chance. I'd call it circumstances really. The policy at the time opened the door.

KH   Yes. So bringing you back to the question, are there things you enjoy about your current job?

HM   The thing I like most is my graduate students really. I just love the intellectual exchange with them. They bring new stuff to me and I to them, and I really enjoy that. I enjoy that kind of one to one communication. So teaching is the best part. I find research really very stressful, and research grants, getting grants, keeping up with all of that, and the politics of work. With the neo-liberal culture of individualism, there isn't a lot of sharing; there isn't a lot of camaraderie and mutual support.

KH   How important do you think work is, in your life?

HM   Well, my partner will tell you that it's far too important, I spend far too much time worrying, and all my waking hours are spent doing it. It consumes me, really.

126

KH   Why do you think that is – that it consumes you?

HM   To stay on top of the food chain, which you are as a professor, you have to keep producing, and you have to keep doing, and you have to keep so many fingers in all the pies. There are high expectations. You've got other responsibilities too like committee responsibilities, and you've got a leadership role. I run a research centre; you've got line management and budgetary responsibilities. You've got lots of things going on at once. You are involved in advisories at policy levels as well your own research and writing. I reckon that if academics were really honest with you – and I don't know if you are interviewing any male academics – there is always this sense in which you always feel everyone else is better than you, and knows more than you. We all walk around with no self confidence at all. I know that's not just me, because I have talked at other levels with other academics, and we all feel the same. We all feel like worms!

KH   Why is that?

HM   I don't know. You are going through the PhD process yourself now, but I think maybe the PhD process is the problem. It is the isolation and the critical wearing down and then proving of yourself which is inherent in the process. It is a rite of passage which is designed to make you feel inferior. You feel like you are going completely nuts! And it continues all the way through the five or so years.

KH   Aagh!

HM   There's a sense in which you never feel complete, you never feel you have the answers, you always feel that the knowledge you are chasing is elusive. Especially now, with the internet where there is so much new information and new research reported every day. You feel – 'how can I keep up with this? I will be found out at any moment that I'm a fraud'. It's not just me, I've talked to other senior academics who say – 'my God, I've been away a few days and everyone will know that I'm not up to date ... what will people think of me?' Or, 'I have to give a paper and it's not going to be good enough'. As an academic you are always feeling you are never good enough. That's something I am sure that begins in the PhD process ... I don't know if people will honestly tell you that.

KH   Yes, it is coming out in my other interviews, a feeling of being a fraud, an interloper, and sometimes they attribute that, perhaps, to class or to gender or to ethnicity ... it's hard to know where to place that in identity terms – or is that a product of the academy, the academic space?

HM   I was watching a tribute programme for John Mortimer the author and playwright who died last night. People close to him were talking about the way he constantly needed reassurance, even though he was so great and prolific. In a sense even though he was from quite an elite, well very middle class, very sort of stable background, there was still a searching that was going on in him, which was never filled. Yet when he was debating in the Oxford Union and when he was presenting law cases as a barrister he was very confident on the outside. He was very funny and witty and he had the social capital to interact and do all those things. So what I am trying to say is I think that it has a lot to do with the nature of the academic beast. The quest for external recognition means that you will always feel never good enough. If he could still feel that way even with all his background, then you've got to be very pompous not to feel that.

KH   Thank you. So you've told me a little bit about your schooling. You went to an all girls' school and then you came back and went to school in Brixton, a secondary school, another all girls' school. You explained a little bit about the careers and picking East Anglia. Did you apply only to the Univesity of East Anglia?

HM   No, I applied to a few others. I can't remember now. This was thirty something years ago. I went in 1977. I did apply to others and went to visit them. I loved visiting them. Oh, it was so great getting on the train and going to places! I felt so free and grown up.

KH   And did you organise it all yourself?

HM   Yes, all by myself because my mum, who was with me at the time because my dad had gone back to Trinidad, didn't know anything about the British education system. In fact, I got myself into the school in Brixton because she didn't know she had to go down to the local authority and put my name down for a school. I did all that myself.

KH   When you were in your university, what did you elect to study? What was the course?

HM   I did Development Studies, which was Third World development. It was a great course. It was Marxist-based and we did things like sociology, anthropology and geography. We had to do land use and go out in the fields and dig potatoes. We had to even do mathematics, statistics and stuff. Economics we had to do too, but we did a critique of neo-classical economics, not just economics. We did development policy, and at that time they hadn't yet done gender in development. By the time I left in the third year, somebody was just beginning to develop a course on it. So gender wasn't part of the programme. But I had one or two inspirational tutors that were women, and felt that if they were lecturers, well, you know, that's pretty normal then to be one. So then it wasn't abnormal to be a woman in university. Though, on reflection, I realise now that they were very junior and they were having a really hard time and they all left! Whereas at the time I just thought they were tutors, and that was brilliant.

KH   Did you feel sort of successful when you were at university?

HM   Successful? Um...I did very well. In my dissertation I got a distinction. But I got married in my first year, and I got pregnant and I had my daughter as I was leaving. In fact I was in advanced pregnancy when I sat my finals and that was really hard, because I got very ill. I had pre-eclampsia and toxemia and I didn't realise it at the time, but the studying and the stress and the diet and not looking after myself, and just working made me very ill. So I could have got a first but I didn't, because I was so ill. But I knew I was good enough. I just knew.

KH   For what?

HM   I knew that I understood things and that I could read things easily, and I wrote good essays, and they were passionate essays. There was a lot of passion in what I was doing. But my marriage was pivotal for me, in my first year of university. I married a strong, devout Muslim, and I converted to Islam. It was the time of the first Muslim uprisings in Iran in the late '70s. I was swept up by the Ayatollah Khomeini and the anti-western, anti-imperialistic dogma. I really found my political voice. I really thought it was all brilliant.

I married my husband and he was very inspirational to me, because, for the first time I felt very politicised. I covered myself, not the full niqab, but with the headscarf and I always wore boots and long skirts. Even though I no longer practice in that way, what I learnt for the first time in my life is the experience of not being treated as a sexual object, to still be a woman but to be seen as myself. I understood what it was to have dignity and respect for myself as a woman. I came from the Caribbean and it was a totally different culture, with carnival and parties and we just did whatever we liked. We wore whatever we liked. So I turned around absolutely, completely, into this very quiet, demure, other person, which actually, subsequently, wasn't me at all. But it taught me about dignity and self respect and about politics, and, you know, about the Palestinian cause and all sorts of things that I had not actually thought about much in my life. So I became quite politicised and quite feminised through Islam.

KH   So, how did you get from finishing university – obviously you were heavily pregnant – to your early career in the academy? What was the pathway?

HM   The pathway was precisely because of that, being pregnant, having a baby and getting married. When we graduated, in those days we had something called the milk round, which I suppose they call work experience now, or maybe other things. But we were really employed by companies then, we weren't just exploited as you are now! I have subsidised multi-nationals for years, with my daughter working for them for free on work experience or internships. In the milk round companies like Marks and Spencer's, McDonalds, or the military would come and recruit graduates. But because my husband and I had a Muslim name we couldn't get a job. I remember writing seventy applications in a month and not getting one reply. We didn't know what to do, and we had a baby. I told you I nearly got a first, but a 2:1 wasn't enough to get a scholarship. You needed a first.

KH   For a PhD?

HM   Yes, for a PhD. I was just at home with the baby and living in real poverty. My husband was doing some casual work, bits and pieces. He was painting the lines on the roads. You know, he's a graduate in economics and politics and he was painting the road! He worked in a bread factory, and he worked in a pizza place, doing all kinds of jobs. I just thought – well, maybe I can go back to college because I can't get a job. This was the '70s; it was overtly racist times. It was very hard. So I just sent my thesis proposal off to Goldsmiths College's sociology department, and it landed on the desk of a particular person, who became my supervisor. He read it and said, 'come and see me'. I said OK. But I couldn't get anyone to look after my daughter, who was eighteen months old then. I had to take her with me, screaming and crying in the pushchair, and I was so distraught myself, because I thought – oh my God, no-one will take me seriously. But he gave me a break. He saw my dissertation, which was on Pakistani pupils in British schools. He thought it was really good, and he put me forward for an ESRC scholarship, and I got it. In those days you could put a dependent down on your grant, and so my husband was my dependent and we had just enough to live on. So the scholarship, actually, was instead of employment for both of us.

KH   Right, so you did your PhD at Goldsmiths. And then what did you do?

HM   Well, I had to suspend halfway through the PhD because I worked as a researcher to make ends meet. I did really well to get a job in a top research centre at the University of London. I met some of the top feminist academics there. It was just amazing, and I was exposed to rigour and I wrote amazing stuff. Some of it was published but wasn't accredited to me though I did all the research and all the writing. That's how you learn about academics! But I realised then that I could really do research, and I just kept going and finished the PhD. It took me five years in all.

Then my supervisor was leaving to go to a university in America. He said: 'there are lots of opportunities for young lecturers there'. I was about to finish and he gave me some cuttings from a newspaper and told me about a job at an Ivy League university in the States. I applied, and I got the job. That was amazing. They flew me over and I had the interviews and everything. So upon finishing my PhD I just got this amazing job in the States. But I couldn't take my daughter with me because of our joint custody arrangements – by then I was divorced.

KH   Right.

HM   I did the job for about a year, thirteen week semesters, coming and going between England and America. I just wasn't happy there. I didn't like it. It was too hard leaving my daughter behind. There were lots of confusing messages for me as a British woman of colour in America in the late 80s. I was single and on my own and there were very closed academic networks. I was also treated like a special case as I was rare as a woman of colour in academia. I wasn't happy, so I came back here to what I knew and understood. After having a tenure track position in an Ivy League university I came back here to work at a tough inner city university. People thought I was crazy!

When I first came back I got a job at my old college, Goldsmiths' doing a big study on crack and cocaine in South London, which catapulted me into the limelight. It was one of the few reports to look at race and ethnicity and drug use and it was very controversial. From there I got a part-time job teaching at South Bank University, a new University in central London. Of course it was a job to teach race and ethnicity to mainly black students! My predecessor was leaving the job and they needed somebody to stand in to teach his courses. Once I was in the job it just kept growing, and I stayed there for nine years. I went from temporary part-time tutor to Head of Sociology, and then Reader. I couldn't have done it without the support of some wonderful women colleagues who mentored me. So I just grew in that system, really.

KH   And you applied for a Chair?

HM   Yes I applied. My first Chair was at Middlesex University in Racial Equality Studies in 1998, over ten years ago. It was a landmark as it was the first Chair in Racial Equality Studies anywhere in the UK and, I have been told, even in the world. It was a very prestigious Chair. It was funded by local government and businesses. So it was a funded tenured Chair.

KH   So why did you apply for it? What made you decide to apply?

HM   I had reached the end of the road in my job at Southbank University. I saw the Ad and I thought, 'that really fits me'. I wouldn't have applied for a Sociology Chair as I wouldn't have felt good enough. But this was so specific, about race equality, and that's what I had done. Also the brief was that they wanted you to work with the local communities. This was something I had done research on, and had really enjoyed, so it was academic as well, not completely academic. It was about good community relations. You had to be a kind of ambassador for the subject as well, which appealed to me a lot. I thought that there weren't many people in the UK who could fit that bill and would stand a chance. But it was competitive and a lot of people were interviewed, but I got it, and it was amazing!

KH   Because of the time I am going to finish off with a few questions on success, just for the last couple of minutes. So first question, if you were giving advice to a younger female academic, what would you say about starting a career?

HM   Well, put it this way, I've always told my daughter – 'don't do it!' I also tell my PhD students, before they start their doctoral studies – think long and hard about what you want and why you are doing it. It is not just about status and being called doctor. Nor should it be an automatic progression after a Masters. It takes you down a particular road and into particular kinds of careers and institutions. You just don't know what the rest of the world can offer you. You are left in this quite narrow world, full of huge egos. So what would I say? I would say if you do a PhD you don't have to end up in higher education like I have. You could take it into other areas. I think I've stayed here because it's what I knew, not because it's what I wanted.

KH   In general terms, what do you think helps to make women successful in the academy?

HM   I don't know how I've got this far, really. A friend of mine said to me you've got to be so ruthless and hard-edged and prolific to survive. I don't see myself as having any of those characteristics, I don't see myself as hard-nosed and a super bitch and, you know...cutting down other people. I just don't see myself like that.

When I was in America, they have a different system there, they have non-academic Deans. When I started I was called in to see the Dean, and she sat me down and she flicked through my papers, barely looking at me. She said: 'well what do you do?' And I said: 'well, I've just written my thesis which was on young black women'. And she said : 'Oh OK, well that's what you will do from now on, young black women, and that's it, you'll specialise, you'll be known for that'. You see, in the States they want you to be known for one thing, not to start being too clever and diversify. Her point was 'you are the one and only expert on young black women'. Somehow that advice just stuck with me, and in fact that's what I am, an expert on young black women. There's no-one who knows more about it than me. And that's what it takes, honing out a niche, making it your own. I think what's really important is mentoring other young women into the subject area. I do that through teaching and through research. So you really hone down, but that doesn't' mean I don't know anything about anything else. You will know about theory and methodology, but you relate it to how it relates to young black or Asian women. I think it's having that niche that no-one else knows as much about which is important for your survival.

KH   Yes, absolutely. Others I have interviewed for my research have talked of a niche, as well. So what is your price of success? What do you feel you paid for your position here?

HM   I think I paid with my creativity. I just feel that I haven't done anything creative. I can paint, I can draw, I can cook, dance, ...I think my health has suffered too, from the stress, and I'd give it up tomorrow and go back to Art College. I'd be happier than being successful, because I don't enjoy this success. You caught me on a bad day, my first day back.

I have a mentor here at the university and both she and my partner say that I have to learn to work within this job, not to give it so much, so that I can do some of my other things that I want to do. I need to take some time off and do my painting or my creative writing, or dancing or other things. I have been quite ill with breast cancer and I reckon that it's had a lot to do with the stress of this job. I promised myself a few years ago when I had it, that I wouldn't go back to the manicness of all that you have to do. But I have! I slipped straight back into it, because to stay on top you have to work really, really hard. I work all weekends, I write, I stay up late, sometimes two or three in the morning, just to get things finished. Maybe I'm a bit of a perfectionist, but it doesn't give me pleasure anymore.

I have just come back from Trinidad and at the end of the day, when I go back home, everyone says – 'oh well done, we've heard about your fabulous inaugural lecture,' and my mum's showing everyone the pictures. But nobody understands what I really do. All my friends don't know. They are all proud of me but it's meaningless. They can't engage with the subject, and they can say racist things, or sexist things, and I can't, on an everyday level, begin to start preaching to them, or telling them about their post colonial identity and theorise about it all because I would just lose my friends and my family. So I am isolated, really. My colleagues will understand it, but they don't love me. But the people that love me don't understand me. So either way, you can't win. I've heard other working class people say that. You move away, and you can't go back. You cross over the tracks and you are sitting in this never-never-land, where you've got work colleagues, but you don't take them home at night. Unless, of course, you are having an affair, which many of the men do!

KH   So success is ...you almost give a sense that it's ...

HM   It's a sad place. It's sad. It's a sad place, and I'm sure celebrities feel like that too ... Michael Jackson, Madonna, Robbie Williams! But it's a lonely place, because you don't quite belong to a collective, a community of scholars – there's no love lost between you. And you can't go back home either. If I go back home to Trinidad as I have done, they'll say – 'don't come here with your clever ideas'. So I have to be another person back home. My only real sanctuary is the world I have made with my closest friends and family here.

KH   So it's negotiation of identities in different contexts and settings?

HM   Yes, and I'm a queen at it, I'm fabulous at it, I can really move between the worlds. You know, ironically, the art of communication is something that most academics lack. But I've had to really develop it to survive, because I'm like two different people. I speak like this now, I speak posh to you and I don't speak in my down homey Trini way. I learnt to do that when they told me that I don't speak English when I applied for my school in Brixton. They said they would take me if I learnt to speak English, and I *was* speaking English! So I've learnt to adapt myself. I learnt how to move between worlds. I've noticed that many successful women of colour, Caribbean and Asian, that's what they do. They compromise, they change themselves, they are one thing, then another thing. It's an art to move in out of the cupboard!

KH   Thank you so much.

Conclusion: Heidi Safia Mirza

In talking to Kate about my academic journey I realise I position my PhD as a pivotal moment in my academic career. However, in the interview I do not talk much about the content and experience of my PhD studies. I unconsciously focus more on the influences that drove me to that point and shaped the opportunities that opened up the space for me to do it. The absence/presence of the PhD is symbolic. Its silence speaks of its situated status as 'just another event' in my educational life history. It seems it is one part of the trajectory toward academic success – a means to an end, a piece of the career puzzle.

The individuated experience I narrate about coming to the PhD and moving beyond it into an academic career is more complex than it may seem at first sight. In my personal story I do not focus on formal structures and institutions, but how I lived it in the everyday. Race, class, gender, sexuality and religion collide in my narrative to create a holistic story of embodied intersectionality (Mirza, 2009). Embodied intersectionality as a concept seeks to make sense of the black woman's symbolic and narrative struggle over the defining materiality of her experience. It provides an intersectional analysis where race, class, gender, and other social divisions are theorised as lived realities.

I articulate my embodied story as a black ethnicised/othered woman through the language of personal success, aspiration, and overcoming. I invoke the emotions of joy and sorrow in the telling. What appears in my story to be opportunity, happenchance and choice is not innocent. My journey through to the PhD and into an academic career is structured by my parents' social location and inter-racial positionality in post-war, post-colonial Britain. The ideologies and economics of racism, colonialism and migration, which influence my opportunities and thinking, are embodied and played out in my emerging sexuality, religious awareness and gendered expectations. State policy in higher education in the 1970s opened doors through which I walked hand in hand with the luck and happenchance of meeting generous and exceptional people who mentored and supported me into my PhD and on to my career as a Professor.

In the introduction I asked 'How do class, race and gender distinctions structure my subjectivity as an othered woman of colour in our overwhelmingly dominant white places of teaching and learning?' This interview reveals the multiple ways structures of power operate to reproduce social divisions and educational opportunities. But it also celebrates the power of human agency, my agency, to seize the wonderful happenchance of life and love and friendship along the way.

8
Beginnings and Ends
Helen M Gunter and Barbara Ann Cole

Where are we now?

We begin this chapter with a poem by Karin Oerlemans (2007:28-29) about her doctoral experiences:

Today
Today
Searched seventeen journal articles
Read two books
Found three obscure references
Understood a new concept
And...

I wrote two hundred words today
The sun called me
To come and dance
And smell the roses
And asked my spirit to join the birds in wheeling and diving in the azure sky
But I sat behind my computer screen
With my back to the window
So I would not heed its cry

I wrote two hundred words today
My friend called me
To come and relax
And do a coffee

And asked my soul to join the shoppers hunting bargains in the
lunch time throng
But I sat in my home office
With the phone off the hook
So I would not hear her call

I wrote two hundred words today
My children called me
To come and play
And build towers
And asked my body to join in the game of hide and seek and let's pretend
But I sat at my desk
With the door closed tight
So I would not feel their joy

I wrote two hundred words today
My supervisor rang
And how I went
How did I go?
And wondered about the progress I made in the writing of my endless
theme
And I told her with pride
That I felt I'd achieved
'I'm really going along,
Today...'

As we complete this collection of 'evocative narratives' (Ellis and Bochner, 2000:744), we want to acknowledge the personal and individual nature of the experience of doing a doctorate and being a doctoral student. Like Sikes (2009), we know that using and promoting such a methodology is challenging for the espoused 'science' that the academy is built on. Nevertheless, as Sikes goes onto argue:

> ...auto/biographical approaches also remind us of the significance of the individuals, of the importance of the personal, without which the collective could not be. Herein lies their power to unsettle some of the foundations on which the academy is based! (p169)

So what Griffiths (2003) calls 'little stories' are important because '...it links voice to narrative by taking the particular perspective of an individual seriously: that is, the individual as situated in particular circumstances in all their complexity'. But we are also mindful of Griffith's alarm bell that: 'telling one's story may help in self-realisation but may also be an exercise in self-delusion. Voice has to be treated with the same criticality as other autobiographical expressions...' (2003: 81-82). So in this final chapter we will recognise the validity of the individual stories but also examine sameness and difference and, importantly, we will give recognition to the bigger picture in which the reported lives have been lived and emplotted within this text.

Oerlemans shows how intense the doctoral process is, not least the choices made at the interface between life as a student and life in general. In this sense doing a doctorate is a personal journey, it is the individual who registers for the degree, who is allocated a supervisor, who writes the thesis, who goes through the viva and who is awarded the degree. Consequently, the doctorate is based on the capacity to exercise agency, to frame and carry out a research project, and to write it up in ways that show a contribution to knowledge that is of publishable standard. Progress can be rapid and slow, writing can flow and be of a dazzling standard and it can be tortuous and bland – all in the same day.

In her chapter Barbara talks about the final stressful rush to finish and print the text in the midst of teaching abroad and having painful toothache; while others talk about the complexity of interplaying family with work and study, where Jennifer talks about how she 'wept silently' through the troubles in which her thesis writing was located. The thesis becomes and remains – even after graduation – a member of the family. So while much depends on agency, it is the structures that shape and control our capacity to exercise agency that matter, and a doctoral student cannot be successful without being able to juggle a range of demands on their time, not least partners and children who expect to be loved and cuddled. It is a long process that demands a huge amount of commitment from partner and family. At this point we could stop, as many books on 'how to do a PhD' focus a lot on the technical side of what needs to be done, with advice on how to do it. However time management and having sufficient emotional intelligence to carry you through the tough times will only get you so far in thesis writing. We did not want to produce such a text, because for ourselves the actual technical delivery of the thesis is only one part of the story.

Doctoral study impacts on a person's life in ways that may not be fully apparent at the time. As a group of prospective authors for this book we got together, each told our story, recognised differences and sameness, and the emerging themes. So in this book we have asked each other to do what Penny calls 'memory work'. In doing so we have told the story not so much of thesis production but of how the thesis is located in our lives and the issues surrounding that. We think this matters. We are not seeking to elicit sympathy or congratulations on getting through. The more we talk about this, the more the realities of knowledge production are opened up to scrutiny, and the more we can begin to understand the relationship between learning and life. There is much to be said about what knowledge and forms of knowing count and who are regarded as legitimate knowers. This is not about the sanctity of the new theory or the original piece of work, but about whether we, in Bourdieu's (1990) terms, know the game in play, whether we want to play it, can play it and want to change it. Not least because the stories are inflected with confidence reducing internal voices of 'can I do this?' and 'should I be doing this?'

This is crucial because others will comment on our work both formally and informally, and even if they don't know what it is about, they will have a view and will give advice that can both enable but also deflate. This does not go away, even though we have played the game and secured top of the tree positions in the higher education hierarchy. Like Gunter and Fitzgerald (2007) we recognise that while people may assume that we are now at the centre of things, in reality we continue to experience peripheral marginality. Consequently we intend to adopt Holland and Lave's (2001) approach to understanding narrative production to analyse the texts where we have emplotted a story of our experiences. In doing this we speak from a standpoint that there is no formal beginning or end, while registration and graduation may provide vivid and necessary organisational boundaries to a doctoral project and thesis, in reality the antecedence of a study and ongoing trajectory from the study is a life's work. It lives in our pasts and our futures, and is deeply embodied. It is evident in our posture, our emotions, our language and our being.

What do we know about ourselves?

We take from Holland and Lave that who we are is never settled, but that it is a social practice where 'we 'author' the world and ourselves in that world' (2001:10). Thus, the 'history in person' (p5) idea is helpful because we recognise that our place within an institution such as a university through doctoral registration is not necessarily equivalent to our place as a person. The interplay between the two means that there are struggles as the two come together at the desk, in the making of choices and in understanding who we are. We have shaped the PhD process through who we are, as well as being shaped by it. Our multiple responsibilities as student, partner, mother, employee, citizen, daughter, are not fixed categories into which we move during a day but are always in play, where our identities are dialogic (Holland and Lave 2001:9). While Oerlemans' (2007) image of the lone student at her desk making choices about study and other activities is a powerful one, and easily recognisable, it is our contention that the individualisation of the doctorate is by its very nature a social process.

Holland and Lave (2001) talk about boundaries where we can try to live our lives separate from others, but we inevitably involve others with whom we present the self every day. There are power processes involved, where power can be exercised over us and with us and by us. Again, to use Holland and Lave (2001), we have all shown examples of 'selves formed in and against uncomfortable practices that they cannot simply refuse' and 'selves formed in and against practices that afford them privilege' (p18). So writers in this text have experienced both oppression and emancipation in their lives, and within the doctoral process this has sometimes been simultaneous – the dialogics of identity have been the place where individuals recall that conscious learning has happened. For example, Heidi talks about how racism prevented her and her husband from getting jobs but how an academic gave her the opportunity to study for a doctorate with a studentship grant.

So the chapters make visible the history within and about the person, in ways that are not settled. While for the purpose of this book the stories are complete, they are not complete for the authors, as we all expect that we will continue to reveal aspects of the role of the doctorate in transforming our lives as we live them. The contexts in which we live now and will live will continue to help us understand the role of intellectual work in enabling us to think and act differently and also in the same ways. There are a number of themes we think essential to engaging with this notion: significantly, how we came to be doing a PhD and how we did it.

All of us talk about the unexpected nature of finding ourselves registered for the PhD. There is strong evidence of coming from backgrounds where attending higher education was not normal and of routes into higher education that do not fit the linear patterns of education systems or the smiling faces looking out to us from university brochures and websites. There is a powerful emotional connection with study: by studying gender Penny wanted to give something back after rebuilding her life; for Jennifer it was the opportunity to take forward her skills and knowledge as a teacher, trade union leader and activist through a post colonial study; for Barbara the lived contradictions of policy around educational inclusion and the standards agenda stimulated a focus on teachers who have children who are perceived as different; for Helen it is the intellectual and professional field she finds herself in that is the focus of study committed to opening up the purposes and practices for scrutiny. Gloria makes her racialised identity both the object and subject of her project and is committed to handing a better legacy for future generations. And, Heidi in conversation with Kate, outlines her work on the intersectionality of class, race and gender with a view to opening up analysis about institutionalised discrimination. Our studies are deeply located in personal experiences, both good and bad, and the passion for study comes from the interplay between who we are and what we read – and how we recognise silences.

While the starting point is with ourselves, the self is validated through the intellectual tools and conceptualisations generated by study. Penny fell in love with sociology, Helen with Bourdieu, and Barbara with Foucault. The transformation in people's lives lies with the power of theory to stimulate theorising, to generate perspectives and to explain the situation we found ourselves in. As Gloria notes, it is the back and forth between theories and data that is exciting. While we had all experienced and know about oppression, we now had a language, a voice and a platform from which to speak, and we now know that power is operating in our lives in ways that are widespread and institutionalised. Power works through social practices, through what is done every day in ways that are assumed to be normal and accepted. This can be enabling: all the writers show how they had opportunities they grasped in the most unexpected ways. People within the system, usually university teachers, suggested, encouraged and opened up study in ways that our story tellers had not previously realised could be for them.

Yet, power can be debilitating – through the impact of gender for Barbara and Penny, class for Helen, race for Jennifer and Gloria, and the interplay of all three for Heidi. This produces ways of knowing that are valid and can enable research to be lived and pedagogic. All talk of experiences of not fitting in, of being black in a white world, of being working class in a middle class university, and what this means for the construction of identity and self worth. Penny gives examples of the tensions and contradictions this generates, not least through how you come to see yourself as not a proper student, or a fraud who will be quickly found out. Identity work is a risky business, and what the stories show is how silence is used to marginalise and how often this becomes a strategy for living in a world that you don't understand and where you may not be understood.

Why we all decided to do something as unsafe and dangerous as a PhD, with topics that challenged the legitimacy of existing structures, is in many ways quite baffling. It cannot be clearly answered; there is much buried in the stories, but what does shout out is that there is a moment in time where values, ideas, and sheer determination come into play with the structural opportunities that are generated.

What does it mean to have a doctorate?

We are all members of the academy. This is what the PhD has done for us. It is a validation of research competence, demonstrating technical proficiency and making an original contribution to knowledge. Credentials matter in the game of academy membership, where the knowledge production process has its own rules, even mysteries. We have all learned to know this through our experiences – some positive, some negative. However, we also know this is a man's world: the cultures are masculine, with claims for rationality where much is actually about realpolitik. It is a classed, raced and aged world. While we women do climb the organisational ladder, and our PhDs have been a ticket to career development, we know that as game players our position remains limited. And we may challenge the ladder not only because our ability to step onto it and climb it remains tenuous, but also because the social practices surrounding it can be alien. We are located in a troubled and troubling place, and drawing on Lather's (1991) analysis of how we can be situated both 'within' and 'against' (p27). We are most definitely within the academy, with all its privileges and aspirations, but by being there we are also changing the academy because we are against the ways in which people like us can be positioned.

We can understand this quite graphically through a theme that has emerged from within the stories. All the writers are intensely aware that as women they have experienced the conflation of biology with social practices, where, as Connell (2002) states, our bodies and our lives are categorised from birth as 'pink' or 'blue'. We talk about this through recognising what it means to learn to be a good girl. Gloria talks about the 'mask of being a good black girl', Penny talks about being the 'good student', Jennifer talks about the complexity of being a 'good' mother, wife, daughter, sister, aunt and friend, while Barbara develops this by talking about becoming 'good wives and mothers' in ways that are classed because a grammar school girl is good in ways that are different from the working class girls who would be good by becoming factory workers.

Being good is not about achieving for the self through education but about marrying right. As Heidi observes, it is about marrying a lawyer or a doctor. For females being good means focusing on dress and grooming in order to be sexually attractive, but at the same time being passive. Waiting is an essential feature. To be asked out, to be complemented, and to be allowed to participate. In the stories, there is a lot of coping through waiting and this links with the experience of being silenced and the decisions to use silence in order to handle discrimination. Waiting is evident because socially acceptable lives were being played out through marriage, children, and low paid jobs.

However, there is much in the stories that shows that we have had to rework what it means to be good so that a number of us could break out of situations, such as unhappy and abusive relationships at home or at work. There are times when the coping and waiting stops. However, being good and being recognised, and praised for being good, does remain, as being awarded the PhD is an example of being a good girl because we have worked within the system and followed the rules, and we cope with being marginalised in spite of our credentials. Getting the work done is applicable to fieldwork as it is to housework.

What interests us is that even though we have legal rights that protect us from abuse and enable us to gain access to study and to work, it is still the case that problems in everyday lives remain. Rusch and Marshall (2006) are helpful, talking about 'gender filters'. They are describing how people handle gender issues in organisations – university, workplace, home – where...

> the filters appear as reactions or responses to situations where gender equity is a subtext. The responses, based either on explicit reasoning or tacit assumptions, express a value position for gender equity. (2006:232)

There are eight filters, grouped into three categories. First are the filters that are based on anger that such an issue should be raised, alongside denial that it exists. Second are the filters where there is recognition of the problem and claims to support equity can be made but behaviours and decisions are not consistent with this when issues arise. And, third, there are filters where events as 'defining' and 'teachable' moments can lead to learning and change, even by people who operate as the 'outsider within': as a respected colleague but who can 'navigate gendered interactions' (p243).

Our chapters show evidence of experiencing anger and denial over how we have come to be dialogic in our identities. There is evidence of how painful this can be, not least through experiencing colonising and de-colonising processes. As Barbara shows, our roles as women have been defined by the state through how welfare and family are conceptualised, and the state has had to concede the need to establish rights to change such approaches. Nevertheless, as Heidi shows, denial was evident in her own parents, as when her mother hid in the cupboard when her grandfather came to visit so his white daughter-in-law was concealed. Helen talks about denying her right to have a voice. Gloria tells the story of how her best friend referred to children who pushed into the dinner queue as 'those ignorant black bastards', but then denied that this included Gloria – and Gloria herself denied that she wanted to be seen as acceptable by white teachers and friends.

145

The second set of filters operate in ways that are subtle and can be contradictory, but they ensure that gendered practices continue. For example, Heidi describes how the grant and no fee system enabled her to go to university, so that she could afford to study and not worry about getting a part time job or accumulating debt. She recognises that for a short space of time there was the opportunity for people like herself to go on to further study and to make a contribution to society. This opportunity has now gone. So while the commitment to access and the rhetoric of widening participation is evident in government policy, the actual practices necessary to achieve this have been removed.

The third set of filters hold possibilities for change because they can 'disrupt the institutionalised practices, highlight equity as an important value, and frequently modify conduct' (p239). It seems to us that the stories have more evidence of this within them, partly because over time the writers have come to understand the other filters, and are working towards such understandings as past tense experiences. Having learned to be outsiders, often with a sense of being inferior and doing inferior things, what the stories illuminate is how we have learned to be proud of who we are, and how we can work within and against to create the teachable moments. As Penny shows, we can translate our achievements in our personal life into our academic life, and vice versa.

Such productive activism has often to be subtle and considered; we get it right and we get it wrong. Jennifer talks about how new programmes in the Caribbean have been developed, students graduated and the University has not collapsed or had its mission damaged – quite the reverse. Gloria examines her emergent realisations about her identities, and how through her practice she can create her own culture. Barbara talks about how she realised that the texts she was using did not speak to her, and how through her research she has sought to make a contribution to how issues of social justice are researched. Helen identifies how through her work on field mapping and conceptualisation she has been able to give recognition to thinking that is outside the mainstream. Nevertheless, as Heidi shows, how you live this contradictory life is constantly challenging, not least because there may be many teachable moments amongst family and friends which may not always be welcome. Being singled out as different by your own community is problematic and, as Penny shows, the burden of being a role model can weigh heavy.

What comes next?

The simple answer to this is that life is what comes next. While we have achieved a lot in our lives, and we are not alone in acknowledging such accomplishments, we are mindful that the constant interplay between structure and agency means that while we seek to establish our agendas, it remains the case that we are always being scripted and judged. Academia may seem to be as fixed as the buildings that house us but, as Jennifer notes, it remains contested for lots of reasons. Neo-liberal cultures and associated managerialism continue to challenge our values and seek to make us into knowledge brokers who must compete in the market or be redundant. We have read the books and lived the experience of performance targets, and we know the damage this continues to do to our lives. While Heidi links it to her illness, Penny notes the greediness of work and home. Our experiences confirm Blackmore and Sach's (2007) analysis of the way in which we are 'outsiders' in what should be our world but isn't:

> ...as new immigrants they are inside, but as managers, remain on the outskirts of the culture, while bringing priorities. As women, they are 'strangers in a familiar world, dominated by men. Their gender leads to a range of cultural processes of assimilation, ghettoisation, and positioning as the 'other'. (p22)

Audit systems can run counter to productive research cultures, and so, as Heidi notes, you have 'to stay on top of the food chain'. This is perpetuated by endemic concerns about ability, achievement and distinction. Indeed, we might ask if this book will be returned in the Research Excellence Framework in 2013 and, if so, will it be graded at 4*, 3*, 2*, 1* or unclassified? Such are our lives that we have to take this seriously, but such is our commitment to challenging the boundaries that we will continue to publish what matters and not just what can be counted.

We are not the only people who want to ask serious questions about women in the academy and, like Mahony and Zmroczek (1997a), we aim to keep the issues alive. There is much in their edited collection about working class women that resonates with the stories we have written. They identify how class remains a feature in lives but it is also a source of pride, and how 'authors write of their feelings of anger and guilt at being part of the academy, at the same time as being excited by intellectual work' (Mahony and Zmroczek, 1997b: 5). We have found that the issues our stories raise generate similar positions: we are held back but go forward, we are made to feel inferior but we continue to feel secure. How this is studied and theorised is central to our agenda as well, especially the complexities of the scholarship within the academy regarding identity and recognition.

Fraser (2001) illuminates these matters, arguing for a politics of recognition based on justice or 'participatory parity' (p33), and so the claims made in these stories for recognition are relevant to meeting her test: first, 'that the institutionalisation of the majority cultural norms denies them participatory parity' (p35). In our stories there is much to confirm that this has been the case and while there have been important legal cases, there remain structural injustices – women paid less than men for the same job; fewer women and black professors – and cultural injustices relating to the rules of the game.

Second, Fraser maintains 'that the practices whose recognition they seek do not themselves deny participatory parity – to some group members as well as to non-members' (p35). In our stories there is evidence of just how complex this is, particularly how the studies, careers and personal lives are about the individual as a social and socialising person. Furthermore, while we are a group of authors in this book, we are not a social group, but instead the intersectionality in our lives is such that we need to look beyond being biologically women in order to examine who we are and how our lives may or may not have impacted on others.

It seems to us that we have tried to enable others to join the journey with us or to take advantage of the opportunities created by our activity. We do not claim this to be special. We instead maintain that our lives have been rather ordinary in many ways. But there are examples within the narratives told here, as well as in the lives of readers, of how sometimes our own achievements in finding new ways of doing things can bring advantages to others. We will probably never know if others have been disadvantaged as a result, and it would be helpful to our learning process if such stories were made available.

What we are saying is that this book could be portrayed as the stories of the privileged few who have broken through and got their recognition through a doctorate. It seems that we have learned the rules of the game and used them to write the stories and have them published. This reading of the stories could be made through a retrospective claim of success, but we have positioned ourselves as people who did not set out to do that, in a world where success is open to interpretation, and where we could have been elsewhere and very happy being there. The struggle for what Fraser calls 'participatory parity' is about lived lives that were and are complex. There has been planning and there has been serendipity but, importantly, there has been personal experience that has been storied in ways that demonstrate how the person takes and creates opportunities, and deals with adversity, or doesn't. And that show how values developed through family life and just sheer living have helped to shape what has been done, what might have been done, and what might happen next.

Consequently, we want to begin from a position of equity, where we are worthy to be in the academy and we can filter the difficult encounters through how we define and act on those moments. This is what will fill our lives and work as we move on. For one thing, it is optimistic and connects with our sense of agency, which has been revealed through these stories. We hope that others will be encouraged to write their stories. We need more studies about what it means to be a man in a man's world, to be white in a white world, to be middle class in a middle class world, to be heterosexual in a heterosexual world. While we women may often be fish out of water in the academy, what we don't know enough about is what it means to be 'a 'fish in water' because 'it does not feel the weight of the water, and it takes the world about itself for granted' (Bourdieu and Wacquant, 1992:127). Such a project would be illuminating, as it would generate teachable moments for us all.

In thinking about such projects and engaging with change agendas that seek to enable lives rather than produce audit data, we take sustenance from Arendt (2000a:181) and her statement:

> without action, without the capacity to start something new and thus articulate the new beginning that comes into the world with the birth of each human being, the life of man, spent between birth and death, would indeed be doomed beyond salvation.

References

Action on Access. (2008, 06-09-2007). 'Higher Education Outreach: Targeting disadvantaged learners.' Retrieved 21 May, 2009, from http://www.actiononaccess.org/index.php?p=2_5_4_3_10

Akbar, N (1995) *Natural Psychology and Human Transformation*, Mind Production and Assoc; Revised Edition

Akbar, N (1985) *The Community of Self*, Mind Production and Association, USA

Apple, M (1993) Series Editor's Introduction. In Casey, K *I Answer with My Life*. New York: Routledge

Archer, L (2003) *Race, Masculinity and Schooling: Muslim boys and education*. Berkshire: Open University Press

Archer, L, Hutchings, M, Leathwood, C and Ross, A (2003) Widening participation in higher education: Implications for policy and practice. In Archer, L Hutchings, M and A Ross (eds) *Higher Education and Social Class: Issues of exclusion and inclusion*. London: Routledge Falmer

Archer, L and Leathwood, C (2003) Identities, inequalities and higher education. In Archer, L, Hutchings, M and Ross, R ((eds) *Higher Education and Social Class: issues of exclusion and inclusion*. London and New York: Routledge Falmer

Arendt, H (2000) *The Portable Hannah Arendt*. Baehr, P (ed) London: Penguin Books

Arendt, H (2000a) Labor, Work, Action. In: Baehr, P. (ed) (2000) *The Portable Hannah Arendt*. London: Penguin Books. pp: 167-181

Armistead, W (1848/1999) *A Tribute for the Negro: being a vindication of the moral, intellectual, and religious capabilities of the coloured portion of mankind; with particular reference to the African race*. http://docsouth.unc.edu/neh/armistead/armistead.html

Arnot, M, David, M and Weiner, G (1999) *Closing the Gender Gap: postwar education and social change*. Cambridge: Polity Press

Asher, N (2009) Writing home/decolonizing text(s). *Discourse: studies in the cultural politics of education*. 30(1) p1-13

Bajunid, I (2000) Rethinking the work of teachers and school leaders in an age of change. In Day, C, Fernandez, A; Hauge, T and Moller, J (eds) *The Life and Work of*

Teachers: international perspectives in changing times. London and New York: Falmer Press

Bales, K (1999) *Disposable People: new slavery in the global economy,* University of California Press, USA

Ball, S (1987) *The Micro-Politics of the School.* London: Methuen

Ball, S (1990) *Politics and Policy Making in Education.* London: Routledge

Ball, S (2001) Better Read: theorizing the teacher. In Dillon, J and Maguire, M (eds) *Becoming a Teacher: Issues in secondary teaching.* Buckingham: Open University Press

Banton, M (1997) *Ethnic and Racial Consciousness,* London and New York: Longman

Barton, L (1998) Markets, Managerialism and Inclusive Education. In Clough, P and Barton L (eds) *Managing Inclusive Education: From Policy to Experience.* London: Paul Chapman Publishing

Bartky, S L (1990) *Femininity and Domination.* London: Routledge

Bennett, A (1994) *Writing Home.* London: Faber and Faber

Bernstein, B (1971) On the classification and framing of educational knowledge. In Young, M (ed) *Knowledge and Control.* Basingstoke: Collier-Macmillan

Blackmore, J (2006) Unprotected participation in lifelong learning and the politics of hope: a feminist reality check of discourses around flexibility, seamlessness and learner earners. In Leathwood, C and Francis, B (eds) *Gender and Lifelong Learning: critical feminist engagements.* Oxon: Routledge

Blackmore, J. and Sachs, J. (2007) *Performing and Reforming Leaders: gender, educational restructuring and organizational change.* Albany, NY: State University of New York Press

Bourdieu, P (1988) *Homo Academicus.* Cambridge: Polity Press

Bourdieu, P (1990) *In Other Words.* Cambridge: Polity Press

Bourdieu, P (2000) *Pascalian Meditations.* Cambridge: Polity Press

Bourdieu, P and Wacquant, L J D (1992) *An Invitation to Reflexive Sociology.* Cambridge: Polity Press

Bravette, G (1993) Liberating Human Potential: Black women managers and emancipator action research. MBA Dissertation (unpublished) South Bank Polytechnic: London.

Bravette, G (1997) Towards Bicultural Competence: researching for personal and professional transformations, Unpublished PhD Thesis, University of Bath, UK

Brereton, B (1985) *Social Life in the Caribbean 1838-1938.* Oxford: Heinemann Educational Publishers

Brereton, B (1986) *A History of Modern Trinidad 1783-1962.* Port of Spain: Heinmann Educational Books

Brine, J (2006) Locating the learner within EU policy: trajectories, complexities, identities. In Leathwood, C and Francis, B (eds) *Gender and Lifelong Learning: critical feminist engagements.* Oxon: Routledge

Burke, P J (2002) *Accessing Education: effectively widening participation.* Stoke-on-Trent: Trentham Books

Burke P J (2006) Fair access? Exploring gender, access and participation beyond entry to higher education, in Leathwood, C and Francis, B (eds) *Gender and Lifelong Learning: critical feminist engagements.* Oxon: Routledge

Burke, P J. (2008) Writing, power and voice: access to and participation in higher education. *Changing English,* 15(2), p199-210

Burke, P J (2009) Men Accessing Higher Education: Theorising continuity and change in relation to masculine identities. *Higher Education Policy* Vol 22 p81-199 July 2009

Burke, P J and Hermerschmidt, M (2005) Deconstructing academic practices through self-reflexive pedagogies. In Street, B (ed) *Literacies Across Educational Contexts: mediating learning and teaching.* Philadelphia: Caslon Press

Burke, P J and Jackson, S (2007) *Reconceptualising Lifelong Learning: feminist interventions.* London: Routledge

Butler, J (1997) *The psychic life of power.* Stanford: Stanford University Press

Butt, R, Raymond, D, McCue, G, and Yamagishi, L (1992) Collaborative Autobiography and the Teacher's Voice. In Goodson, I.F. (ed) *Studying Teachers' Lives.* New York: Teachers College Press

Campbell, C (1987) The Teachers' Protests. In Thomas, R (ed) *The Trinidad Labour Riots of 1937: perspectives 50 years later.* Trinidad and Tobago: Extra Mural Studies, University of the West Indies

Campbell, C (1997) *Endless Education: main currents in the education system of modern Trinidad and Tobago 1939-1986.* Mona: The Press, University of the West Indies

Campbell, J (2003) *The Hero's Journey: Joseph Campbell on his life and work,* 3rd edition, Cousineau, P (ed) Novato, California: New World Library

Carnell, E, MacDonald, J, McCallum, B and Scott, M (2008) *Passion and Politics. Academics reflect on writing for publication.* London: Institute of Education

Carr, W (1995) *For Education: towards critical educational Inquiry.* Buckingham: Open University Press

Casey, K (1993) *I Answer with My Life.* New York: Routledge

Casey, K (1995) The new narrative research in education. *Review of Research in Education* 21 p211-253

Clancy, K (1997) Academic as Anarchist: Working class lives into middle-class culture. In Mahony, P and Zmroczek, C (eds) *Class Matters: working class women's perspectives on social class.* London: Taylor and Francis

Clandinin, J (ed) (2007) *Handbook of Narrative Inquiry: mapping a methodology.* Thousand Oaks California: Sage

Clandinin, D J and Connelly, F M (1994) 'Personal experience methods' in Denzin, NK and Lincoln, Y S (eds) *Handbook of Qualitative Research.* Thousand Oaks, California: Sage

Clegg, S and David, M (2006) Passion, pedagogies and the project of the personal in higher education. *Twenty-First Century Society.* 1(2), p149-165

Coffey, A (1999) *The Ethnographic Self: Fieldwork and the Representation of Identity.* London: Sage Publications

Cole, B A (2002) Mothers, teachers and 'special' children: a narrative inquiry into the lives of mother-teachers of children with special educational needs. Unpublished thesis Keele University

Cole, B A (2004) *Mother-Teachers: insights into inclusion.* London: David Fulton Publishers

Collins, P (2000) *Black feminist thought: knowledge, consciousness, and the politics of empowerment.* London: Routledge

Connell, R W (2002) *Gender.* Cambridge: Polity Press

Cosslett, T, Lury, C and Summerfield, P (eds) (2000) *Feminism and Autobiography: texts, theories, methods.* London and New York: Routledge

Crenshaw, K (1989) Demarginalizing the Intersection of Race and Sex: a black feminist critique of antidiscrimination doctrine, feminist theory and antiracist politics. *University of Chicago Legal Forum* 14 p538-554

David, M. (1993a) *Parents, Gender and Education Reform*, Cambridge: Polity Press.

David, M. (2000) 'A Feminist Sociology of family life: Family and Education in [Academic] Women's lives, in Paper presented at the British Educational Research Association Annual Conference, Cardiff University, 7-9 September 2000.

David, M (2003) *Personal and the Political: feminisms, sociology and family lives.* Stoke on Trent: Trentham Books

Davies, B (1997) The Subject of Post-structuralism: a reply to Alison Jones. *Gender and Education,* 9(3), p271-283

Davies, B (2006) Subjectification: the relevance of Butler's analysis for education. *British Journal of Sociology of Education,* 27(4), p425-438

Davis, K (2008) Intersectionality as buzzword: a sociology of science perspective on what makes a feminist theory successful. *Feminist Theory,* 9 p67-85

Deem, R. (1996) Border Territories: a journey through sociology, education and women studies. *British Journal of Sociology of Education.* 17 (1) p5-19.

Denzin, N K (1989) *Interpretive Biography.* Thousand Oaks, California: Sage

DES (Department of Education and Science) (1978) *Special Educational Needs: Report of the Committee of Enquiry into the Education of Handicapped Children and Young People (The Warnock Report),* London: HMSO

DES (Department of Education and Science) (1981) *Circular 8/81 The Education Act 1981,* London: DES

DES (Department of Education and Science) (1988) *Draft Circular [1/89] Revisions of Circular 1/83. Assessments and Statements of Special Educational Needs; Procedures within the Education, Health and Social Services,* London: DES

DfEE (Department for Education and Employment) (1994) *The Code of Practice on the Identification and Assessment of Special Educational Needs*, London: HMSO

DfEE (Department for Education and Employment) (1997a) *Excellence for All Children: Meeting Special Educational Needs*, London: DfEE

DfEE (Department for Education and Employment) (1997b) *The SENCO Guide*, London: DfEE

DfEE (Department for Education and Employment) (1997c) *Excellence in Schools*, London: DfEE

DfEE (Department for Education and Employment) (1998a) *Meeting Special Educational Needs: A Programme of Action*, London: DfEE

DfEE (Department for Education and Employment) (1999) *Learning to Succeed – a new framework for post-16 learning.* London: The Stationery Office

DfES (Department for Education and Skills (2001) *Special Educational Needs Code of Practice*, London: DfES

DfES (2003) *The Future of Higher Education.* London, The Stationery Office Ltd

DfES (Department for Education and Skills) (2002) *Special Educational Needs: a mainstream issue*, London: Audit Commission's Report

DfES (Department for Education and Skills) (2004) *Removing Barriers to Achievement: The Government's Strategy for SEN*, London: DfES

Diamond, J (1999) Access: The year 2000 and beyond – what next? *Journal of Access and Credit Studies.* Summer 1999, p183-191

ECU (Equality Challenge Unit) (2008) *Equality in Higher Education Statistical Report 2008.* London: Equality Challenge Unit

Edwards, R (1993) *Mature Women Students: separating or connecting family and education.* London: Taylor and Francis

Ellis, C and Bochner, A (2000) Autoethnography, personal narrative, reflexivity: researcher as subject. In Denzin, N K and Lincoln, Y S (eds) *Handbook of Qualitative Research* (2nd edn) p733-768

Emihovich, C (1995) Distancing passion: narratives in social science. In Hatch, J A and Wisniewski, R (eds) *Life History and Narrative*, London: The Falmer Press

Fanon, F (1967) *Black Skin White Masks.* New York: Grove Press

Fitzgerald, T and Gunter, H M (2005) Trends in the administration and history of education: what counts? A reply to Roy Lowe. *Journal of Educational Administration and History.* 37 (2) p127-136

Fitzgerald, T and Gunter, H M (eds) (2009) *Educational Administration and History: the state of the field.* London: Routledge

Foucault, M (1984) The Means of Correct Training (from *Discipline and Punish*). In P. Rabinow (ed) *The Foucault Reader.* London, Penguin Books

Frankenberg, R (1993) *The Social Construction of Whiteness: white women... race matters.* University of Minnesota Press

Fraser, N (1997). *Justice Interruptus: Critical reflections on the 'Postsocialist' condition.* London: Routledge

Fraser, N (2001) Recognition without ethics? *Theory, Culture and Society* 18 (2-3) 21-42

Freire, P (1985) *The Politics of Education.* New York: Bergin and Garvey

Fulcher, G (1999) *Disabling Policies? A comparative approach to education policy and disability.* Sheffield: Phillip Armstrong

Gillborn, D and Youdell, D (2000) *Rationing Education: policy, practice, reform and equity.* Buckingham: Open University Press

Giroux, H (1998) Youth, memory work, and the racial politics of whiteness. In J Kincheloe, S Steinberg, N Rodriguez and R Chennault (eds). *White Reign: Deploying, Whiteness in America.* New York: St Martins Press

Goodson, I (2000) Professional knowledge and the teacher's life and work. In Day, C; Fernandez, A; Hauge, T and Moller, J (eds) *The Life and Work of Teachers: international perspectives in changing times.* London and New York: Falmer Press

Goodson, I and Sikes, P (2001) *Life History Research in Educational Settings: learning from lives.* Buckingham: Open University Press

Gordon, G (2006) Transforming Thinking Amongst British African Caribbeans as an Academically Based Community Service Contribution. *Journal of Transformative Education.* Vol 4(3) p226-242

Gordon, G (2007) *Towards Bicultural Competence: beyond Black and White*, Stoke-on-Trent: Trentham Books

Gorelick, S (1991) Contradictions of feminist methodology. *Gender and Society* 5(4) p459-477

Grace, G (1978) *Teachers, Ideology and Control: a study in urban education.* London: Routledge and Kegan Paul

Gramsci, A (1971) *Selections from the Prison Notebooks.* London: Lawrence and Wishart

Greenfield, T (1978) Where does the self belong in the study of organisation? Response to a symposium. *Educational Administration.* 6 (1) p81-101

Greenfield, T and Ribbins, P (eds) (1993) *Greenfield on Educational Administration.* London: Routledge

Griffiths, M (2003) *Action for Social Justice in Education.* Maidenhead: Open University Press

Gullestad, M (1996) *Everyday Life Philsophers.* Oslo: Scandinavian University Press

Gunter, H M (1997) *Rethinking Education: the consequences of Jurassic management.* London: Cassell

Gunter, H M (1999) An intellectual history of the field of educational management from 1960. Unpublished PhD thesis, Keele University

Gunter, H.M. and Fitzgerald, T. (2007) The contribution of researching professionals to field development: introduction to the special edition. *Journal of Educational Administration and History*. 39 (1) p1-16.

Gunter H M and Forrester G (2008) *Knowledge Production in Educational Leadership Project.* Final report to the ESRC. RES-000-23-1192

Gunter, H M and Ribbins, P (2003) The field of educational leadership: studying maps and mapping studies, *British Journal of Educational Studies*, 51 (3) p254-281

Gunter, H M and Willmott, R (2002) Biting the Bullet, *Management in Education*, 15 (5) p35-37

Habermas, J (1972) *Knowledge and Human Interests.* (Trans. J. Shapiro). London: Heinemann

Hall, S (2000) Who needs 'identity'. In du Gay, P and Redman R (eds) *Identity: a reader.* London: Sage

Hammersley, M (2003) Recent Radical Criticism of Interview Studies: any implications for the sociology of education? *British Journal of Sociology of Education* 24(1) p119-126

Hatch, J A and Wisniewski, R (eds) (1995) *Life History and Narrative.* London: The Falmer Press

HEFCE (2006) *Widening Participation: a review.* Higher Education Funding Council for England

HESA (Higher Education Statistics Agency) 2007/8 On line http://www.hesa.ac.uk/index.php?option=com_datatables&Itemid=121&task=show_category&catdex=3#Table_0b_

Holland, D and Lave, J (2001) History in Person: An Introduction. In: Holland, D and Lave, J (eds) *History in Person: enduring struggles, contentious practices, intimate identities.* Santa Fe: School of American Research Press

hooks, bel (2000) *Feminist theory: from the margin to the centre.* Cambridge, MA: South End Press

Jones, A (1993) 'Becoming a 'Girl': post-structuralist suggestions for educational research. *Gender and Education*, 5(2), p157-165

Jones, R and Thomas, L (2005) The 2003 UK Government Higher Education White Paper: a critical assessment of its implications for the access and widening participation agenda. *Journal of Education Policy*, 20(5), p615-630

Josselson, R and Lieblich, A (eds) (1999) *Making Meaning of Narratives.* Thousand Oaks, California: Sage

Kritzman, L D (ed.) (1988) *Michel Foucault: Politics, philosophy and culture- interviews and other writings* (1977-1984). Translator Alan Sheridan and others, New York: Routledge

Kendall, G and Wickham, G (1999) *Using Foucault's Method.* London: Sage Publication

Kirsch, G (1999) *Ethical Dilemmas in Feminist Research: the politics of location, interpretation and publication.* Albany: State University of New York Press

Kotre, J (1983) *Outliving the Self: how we live on In future generations.* W W Norton and Company: New York and London

Larson, E. (1998) Reframing the Meaning of Disability to Families: The Embrace of Paradox. *Social Science and Medicine.* Vol.47 (7), p865-75

Lather, P (1991) *Feminist Research in Education: Within/Against.* Geelong: Deakin University

Lavia, J (2004) Education policy and teacher professionalism in Trinidad and Tobago in a period of transition: 1956-1966. Unpublished PhD Thesis, University of Sheffield UK

Lavia, J (2006) Reflections on doing educational research in a postcolonial setting. In Reiss, M; De Palma, R and Atkinson, E (eds) *Marginality and Difference in Education and Beyond.* Stoke on Trent: Trentham

Leonard, D (2001) *A woman's guide to doctoral studies.* Maidenhead: Open University Press

Lukes, S (1974) *Power: a radical view.* New York: Macmillan

Lyons, N. (2007) Narrative Inquiry: What possible future influence on policy or practice? In Clandinin, J (ed.) *Handbook of Narrative Inquiry: Mapping a Methodology.* Thousand Oaks, London, New Delhi: Sage Publications

MacIntosh, A (1989) Because We Are Human Beings ... Meaning Development, Meaning Metaculture. *The Coracle,* Iona Community, 3 (2), p13-14 'internet version from www.AlastairMcIntosh.com'

Mahony, P and Zmroczek, C (eds) (1997a) *Class Matters: 'Working-Class' women's perspectives on social class.* London: Taylor and Francis

Mahony, P and Zmroczek, C (1997b) Why Class Matters. In: Mahony, P and Zmroczek, C (eds) *Class Matters: 'Working-Class' women's perspectives on social class.* London: Taylor and Francis p1-17

Marcia, J (1966) Development and validation of ego-identity status. *Journal of Personality and Social Psychology,* 3, p551-558

Martinas, S (1992) The Culture of White Supremacy. CWS Workshop. http://www.prisonactivist.org/cws/cws-culture.html

McCall, L (2005) The Complexity of Intersectionality. *Signs* 30 (3) p1771-800

McCarthy, C (1998) *The Uses of Culture: Education and the limits of ethnic affiliation.* New York: Routledge

McCulloch, G; Helsby, G and Knight, P (2000) *The Politics of Professionalism: teachers and the curriculum.* London: Continuum

McLaughlin, J., Goodley, D., Clavering, E. and Fisher, P. (2008) *Families Raising Disabled Children Enabling Care and Social Justice.* New York NY: Palgrave MacMillan

McWhorter, J (2001) *Losing the Race: self-sabotage in black America.* Perennial: New York

Middleton, S (1995) Doing Qualitative Educational Research in the Mid-1990s: issues, contexts and practicalities. Keynote address to the 1995 Conference of New Zealand Association for Research in Education, University of Waikato

Middleton, S and May, H (1997) *Teachers Talk Teaching 1915-1995.* Palmerston North: The Dunmore Press

Miliband, R (1973) *The State in Capitalist Society.* London: Quartet Books

Mills, C Wright (1959) *The Sociological Imagination.* NY: Oxford University Press,

Mills, C (1970) *The Sociological Imagination.* Harmondsworth: Penguin Books

Mirza, H S (2009) *Race, Gender and Educational Desire: why black women succeed and fail.* London: Routledge

Morley, L (1997) A class of one's own: Women, social class and the Academy. In Mahony, P and Zmroczek, C (eds) *Class Matters. working class women's perspectives on social class.* London: Taylor and Francis Ltd

Morley, L (1999) *Organising Feminisms: the micropolitics of the academy.* Hampshire: Macmillan Press

Morley, L (2003) *Quality and Power in Higher Education.* Berkshire, England and Philadelphia: Society for Research in Higher Education and Open University Press

Mumford, L (1956) The Transformation of Man, edited by Ruth Nanda Anshen, Harper and Brothers, NY in *Psychosynthesis Research Foundation Newsletter* 29, December, 1966, http://www.aap-psychosynthesis.org/resources/articles/NewslettersPRF.pdf

Murray, P (2003) Reflections on Living with Illness, Impairment and Death. *Disability and Society,* Vol.18 (4) p.523-6

Murray, P (2000) Disabled Children, Parents and Professionals: Partnership on Whose Terms? *Disability and Society,* Vol.15 (4) p.683-98

Oakley, A (1974) *The Sociology of Housework.* Allen Lane, London: Penguin Books

Oerlemans, K (2007) Students as Stakeholders: voices from the antipodes. *Journal of Educational Administration and History,* 39 (1) p17-31

ONS (2003) *Ethnic Group Statistics A Guide for the collection and classification of ethnic data.* HMSO

Oxaal, I (1982) *Black Intellectuals and the Dilemmas of Race and Class in Trinidad.* Cambridge: Schenkman Publishing

Painter, N (1995) *Soul Murder and Slavery: the fifteenth Charles Edmondson historical lectures,* Baylor University, Waco: Texas: Markham Press Fund

Palmer, P (1997) *The Courage to Teach: exploring the inner landscape of a teacher's life.* San Francisco: Jossey-Bass Publishers

Patterson, O (1982) *Slavery and Social Death: a comparative study,* Harvard University Press

Pillay, V (2007) *Academic Mothers.* Stoke-on-Trent: Trentham Books

Pinderhughes, E (1979) Afro-Americans and economic dependency, *The Urban and Social Change Review,* 12 (2) p24-37

Plummer, K (1993) *Documents of Life: an introduction to the problems and literature of the humanistic method.* London: Routledge

Polkinghorne, D E (1988) *Narrative knowing and the human sciences.* Albany: State University of New York Press

Polkinghorne, D E (1995) Qualitative procedures for counselling research. In Watkins, C E and Schneider, L J (eds) *Researching in counselling.* Hillsdale: Erlbaum

Procter, J (2000) Africans and Afro-Caribbeans: a personal view (1984) in *Writing Black in Britain 1948-1998: an interdisciplinary anthropology,* Manchester University Press

Reason, P (2001) The Action Turn: towards a transformational science, http://people. bath.ac.uk/mnspwr/Papers/TransformationalSocialScience.htm

Reay, D (1997) The Double-Bind of the 'Working-Class' Feminist Academic: the success of failure or the failure of success? In Mahony, P and Zmroczek, C (eds) *Class Matters. Working Class Women's Perspectives on Social Class.* London: Taylor and Francis

Reay, D (2005) *Degrees of choice: class, race, gender and higher education.* Stoke-on-Trent: Trentham Books

Reay, D, Davies, J, David, M, and Ball, S (2001) Choices of Degree or Degrees of Choice? Class, 'Race' and the Higher Education Choice Process. *Sociology,* 35(4) p855-87

Richardson, L (1990) *Writing Strategies: reaching diverse audiences.* London: Sage

Robertson, J (1999) Writing and re-writing the self: an 'exbulimic/woman/researcher' researching with 'bulimics. *Auto/Biography* V11(1&2) p69-76

Rusch, E A and Marshall, C (2006) Gender filters and leadership: plotting a course to equity. *International Journal of Leadership in Education.* 9 (3) p229-250

Ryan, S (1971) *Race and Nationalism in Trinidad and Tobago: a study of decolonisation in a multicultural society.* Toronto: University of Toronto Press

Sandelowski, M (1994) The Proof is in the Pottery: toward a poetic for qualitative inquiry' in Morse, J M (ed) *Critical Issues in Qualitative Research Methods.* London: Sage

Sawicki, J (1991) *Disciplining Foucault: feminism, power and the body.* New York and London: Routledge

Schengold, L (1989) *Soul Murder: the effects of childhood abuse and deprivation.* New York: Fawcett Columbine

SCMH (2002) An Executive Briefing on Breaking the Circles of Fear. *Briefing* 17, Sainsbury Centre for Mental Health

Sheldon, A (2004) Women and Disability. In Swain, J French, S Barnes, C and Thomas, C (eds) *Disabling barriers – enabling environments.* London: Sage

Sikes, P (1997) *Parents Who Teach: Stories from Home and from School.* London: Cassell

Sikes, P (2009) The study of teachers' lives and careers: an auto/biographical life history of the genre. In: Satterthwaite, J, Piper, H and Sikes, P (eds) *Power in the Academy.* Stoke-on-Trent: Trentham Books p169-183

Simon, R I (1992) *Teaching Against the Grain: texts for a pedagogy of possibility.* USA: Bergin and Garvey,

Sivanandan, A (1974) Alien Gods, chapter 5 in *Colour, Culture and Consciousness: immigrant intellectuals in Britain*, edited by Bhikhu Parekh, George Allen and Unwin, London

Smith, D (1987) *The Everyday World as Problematic: A Feminist Sociology.* Milton Keynes: Open University Press

Smith, L (1999) *Decolonizing Methodologies: research and indigenous peoples.* London: Zed Books Ltd

Some, S (2008) Welcoming the Soul Home Through Initiation, The Gifts of Intimacy and Wisdom: gifts of elders and youth in evolving our cultural dialogue, *Living Dialogues*, http://www.livingdialogues.com/Sobonfu_Some.html

Sparkes, A (1994) Life histories and the issue of voice: reflections on an emerging relationship. *Qualitative Studies in Education* 7(2) p163-183

Stanley, L (1993) On auto/biography in sociology. *Sociology* 27(1) p41-52

Steedman, C (2001) *Dust.* Manchester: Manchester University Press

Steedman, C (2005) *Landscape for a Good Woman.* London: Virago

Stuart, M (2000) Beyond rhetoric: reclaiming a radical agenda for active participation in Higher Education. In Thompson, J (ed) *Stretching the Academy: the politics and practice of widening participation in Higher Education.* Leicester: NIACE

Thomas, C (1999) *Female Forms: experiencing and understanding disability.* Buckingham: Open University Press

Thomas, D A (1989) Mentoring and Irrationality: the role of racial taboos. *Human Resource Management.* 28 (2) Summer, p279-290

Thompson, J (2000) *Women, class and education.* London: Routledge

Thomson, P and Gunter, H M (2006) From 'consulting pupils' to 'pupils as researchers': a situated case narrative, *British Educational Research Journal.* 32 (6) p839-856

Tisdell, E J (2000) The Politics of Positionality: teaching for social change in Higher Education (chapter 8), *Power in Practice: adult education and the struggle for knowledge and power in society,* Ronald M. Cervero, Arthur L. Wilson and Associates (eds) John Wiley and Sons

Trinidad and Tobago Unified Teachers' Association (1981) TTUTA's Constitution. Curepe, Trinidad: TTUTA

Trinidad and Tobago Unified Teachers' Association (1991) *TTUTA Study Circle: A New Approach to Membership Education.* Curepe: TTUTA

Unesco (2000) Slave Route Newsletter No. 1 September, http://unesdoc.unesco.org/images/0015/001511/151178e.pdf

Van Maanen, J (1988) *Tales of the Field: on writing ethnography.* Chicago: University of Chicago Press

Van Manen, M (1990) *Researching lived experience: human science for an action sensitive pedagogy.* Albany, NY: State University of New York Press

Vanzant, I (2000) *Yesterday I Cried: celebrating the lessons of living and loving.* New York: Fireside

Walcott, D (1986) *A Far Cry from Africa-Collected Poems: 1948-1984.* New York: Noonday

White, S (2009) Mothers becoming teachers. What motivates them? What doesn't? *International Journal of Inclusive Education,* 13(1) p79-92

Williams, E (1962) *History of the People of Trinidad and Tobago.* Port of Spain: People's National Movement Publishing

Williams, J (1997) The discourse of access: the legitimisation of selectivity. In Williams J (ed) *Negotiating Access to Higher Education: the discourse of selectivity and equity.* Buckingham, The Society for Research into Higher Education and Open University Press

Wilson, E (1977) *Women and the Welfare State.* London: Tavistock

Index

163